Chris

May life and love always mix well in you and yours

Richard

(Dr. J. Richard Cookerly)

Recovering Love

Recovering Love

Codependency to CoRecovery®

Dr. J. Richard Cookerly

Human Services Institute
Bradenton, Florida

TAB BOOKS
Blue Ridge Summit, PA

Human Services Institute publishes books on human problems, especially those affecting families and relationships: addiction, stress, alienation, violence, parenting, gender, and health. Experts in psychology, medicine, and the social sciences have gained invaluable new knowledge about prevention and treatment, but there is a need to make this information available to the public. Human Services Institute books help bridge the information gap between experts and people with problems.

FIRST EDITION
FIRST PRINTING

Published by HSI and TAB Books.
TAB Books is a division of McGraw-Hill, Inc.

Library of Congress Cataloging-in-Publication Data

Cookerly, J. Richard.
Recovering love : codependency to corecovery / by J. Richard Cookerly.
p. cm.
ISBN 0-8306-3838-5
1. Codependents—Rehabilitation. 2. Codependents—Family relationships. 3. Love. 4. Marital psychotherapy. I. Title.
RC569.5.C63C66 1992
158′.24—dc20 92-11013
CIP

TAB Books offers software for sale. For information and a catalog, please contact TAB Software Department, Blue Ridge Summit, PA 17294-0850.

Questions regarding the content of this book should be addressed to:

Human Services Institute, Inc.
P.O. Box 14610
Bradenton, FL 34280

Acquisitions Editor: Kimberly Tabor
Development Editor: Lee Marvin Joiner, Ph.D.
Copy Editor: Pat Holliday
Cover Photograph: Susan Riley, Harrisonburg, Virginia HSI

Dedication

This book is dedicated to Kathleen McClaren, my special, endearing and enduring mate who gives me the love this book talks about and whose countless, dedicated efforts on behalf of this volume are living proof of the ancient wisdom: work can be love made manifest in its worthiest form.

Contents

Contents

Acknowledgments

I am thankful for the fine assistance and contributions of all those who have made possible the publication of *Recovering Love*.

Most of all, my eternal gratitude for her extraordinary help goes to my most wonderful partner in life and in this project, Kathleen McClaren. With consistent and ever-needed love, Kathie labored beside me through every iota of this endeavor. She contributed from her fine mind, from her marvelous and sustaining spirit, and from her very special nurturing heart. Every element of this book has benefitted from Kathie's work and without her this volume could not have been created.

I am also grateful to my many colleagues for their support in the development of the CoRecovery Program which was the impetus for this book. I am especially thankful to my fellow therapists and CoRecovery assistants, Ric Nesbit and Carol Darwin, for their support and many efforts in the development of the CoRecovery program. I give special thanks to all the staff and trainees (both past and present) at the Center for Counseling and Developmental Services who contributed to the creation of the outpatient version of CoRecovery. I applaud the very caring and helpful staff of HCA Richland Hospital whose openness to innovation brought about the very first inpatient CoRecovery program.

Many thanks also go to Denise Wilder, Connie Lynn Miller, and Katherine Berryman for long hours of typing and revising, to Bridget Parrish, our computer whiz kid, and Dennis Webb who repeatedly rescued us all from computer chaos. I also give many thanks to Beverly Goldberg whose editing, organizing, and polishing efforts helped us get off to a great start.

Considerable appreciation goes to my friends and relatives who have lovingly understood my "hermit author" existence while writing this book. I am also thankful for the beauty, peace, and refuge of Sandarthia and the spirit that never ceases to reach and renew me there.

I greatly honor the many wonderful clients who have provided me with inspiration, example, hope, valuable insight, and many treasured experiences.

To ensure privacy and confidentiality, I have changed the names and identifying information of all clients and their situations mentioned in the book. The examples I use are in most cases representative composites of many different people with whom I have worked. Their words have been kept essentially in tact, with changes made to preserve their privacy. All cases were chosen because they exemplify numerous typical and repeating situations in the lives of many people.

Introduction

When people ask me how I can sit day after day listening to pain and suffering and problems and tragedy I say, "That's not what I do. Mostly, I get to see victories and healing and growth and the wonderful miracles that people are. I have the best kind of job there is." Yes, in my office we deal with problems but I have seen the "insurmountable" conquered and the "hopeless" cured. I have seen couples make amazing turnarounds from codependency when the concepts and techniques of CoRecovery have been used. The focus of CoRecovery is the way couples can work as a team to identify and defeat the devastating effects of codependency, thereby maintaining and strengthening their relationships instead of ending them.

In the CoRecovery method the new scientifically based knowledge about love is added to recognized knowledge of codependency treatment. Together they provide the tens-of-thousands of codependent couples a way to overcome their problems as a couple. *The success of CoRecovery programs dispels the commonly held notions that codependent relationships can never be changed, that ending the relationship is inevitable and that overcoming codependency is something to be done only from a single-person perspective.*

This book covers a wide variety of problems and behaviors that mark codependency and offers original "couple" solutions based on the new and successful CoRecovery model, tested in hospitals and treatment centers. Some of the special features of this book are *A Couple's Codependency Check List*, many research findings on the good physical health effects of behaving with love, and many practical exercises and case examples. As well as being a self-help text, this book can be used by therapists as an adjunct to their work assisting couples who enter counseling, and by hospitals and treatment centers.

Couples can work past the problems of codependency. By working in the love-based program called CoRecovery, a couple can achieve a pragmatic understanding of how the mysterious thing we call love really works. This knowledge can save lives, sanity, health, and relationships.

Part One

Codependency

Codependency . . . 1

How Did We Get Into This and How Do We Get Out - Together?

"Finally we are happy together! Finally we know what it takes to keep us together as a healthy, loving couple. And finally together we are growing our love instead of destroying it with codependency. It took work and a whole new and better way of understanding how real love functions, but it was sure worth it!" Those are the words of one man who with his mate is among the large and growing number of couples learning to succeed as a team by focusing on new knowledge about love and CoRecovery.

Unfortunately, countless other couples are being destroyed because they don't know how to work as a team. They don't know how to stop the destruction caused by codependent behavior and to create healthful love instead. Consequently, about half of all marriages end in divorce and many other dedicated nonmarital love relationships also break up. Breakups of all kinds are often followed by psychological, economic, social, and even physical destruction. Stress, illnesses, violence, substance abuse, addictions, suicide, and even murder are not uncommon outcomes of the failure of mated love relationships. Some, of course, only suffer mildly disrupted functioning and the stress of change, but most are negatively affected to some degree, many quite seriously. Others, of course, live on in mutually miserable marriages and in conflicted, dysfunctional, and harmful relationships. Marriage counselors sometimes say that only a fourth of all couples can be considered to be functioning healthfully and happily. We have the knowledge to do far better than that. The good news is that a quiet revolution has started in which couples are learning and practicing what it really takes to succeed at love.

You, too, can be part of this revolution in couples' success.

One Couple's Codependency and What They Did About It

Anna and Bob came to the Center for Counseling and Developmental Services as most couples do, having been referred by another couple who had overcome their difficulties with our help. Bob was ready to call it quits and confided he was only coming to achieve a less-than-awful divorce, if possible. Anna was sure she could fix everything if she only knew what to do and tried hard enough, something she was more than willing to do. Both were blind to several very important facts. Their problems had been *co*-created and probably would be *re*-created in new relationships. *The couple's solutions would have to be co-created because one person can seldom, if ever, solve a significant relationship problem alone.* Often in a codependent relationship this is exactly what's attempted. One person tries to solve the problem of the other without either of them seeing they have mutual problems that must be mutually addressed.

Just like one singer cannot make a duet successful, nor one doubles partner in tennis make a winning team, one mate cannot produce a successful couples relationship. It takes two forming harmony, coordination, and teamwork to succeed as a pair.

Bob and Anna, without knowing it, were, in their way, a well-coordinated team. The trouble was they were a team for failure through their codependent relating. In their first joint appointment, I asked Anna and Bob to face each other and to experiment with my coaching their conversation. I suggested they start by asking each other for something they would want from the other within the next week.

Anna frowned and quickly said, "I need you to stop working yourself to death and come home where I can take care of you and you can get some rest, and we can all be together like a family should be." Bob looked pained and began to defend his working late with various excuses. They had already made at least a dozen communication mistakes in almost perfect teamwork. They also showed a classic couple's codependency pattern.

I asked Anna to do something that surprised her. I said, "Anna, would you ask Bob how you help him to want to stay away from home and work late?" Bob looked hopeful. Wide-eyed, Anna asked, "Do I? Do I do things that help you want to stay away?" Bob answered, "Yes, as a matter of fact, you do. To tell the truth, I stay at work as long as possible because I hate to come home. At work I get to take care of myself, to do things my way. I feel in charge of my life. When I come home it all changes, and I feel unacceptable, inadequate, and guilty because you're always saving me from myself and I hate it. I love you, Anna, but I increasingly hate myself when I'm with you, so I stay away a lot."

Then I suggested Anna, who looked surprised and about to make the mistake of defending herself, do another thing. "Anna, would you ask Bob how he helps you keep doing all those things he doesn't like?" Bob looked puzzled. "Yes, Bob," Anna said. "Do you know what you do that helps me keep doing all that?" Bob started slowly. "Well, first I guess I never told you I stay at work just to avoid your caretaking ways. I never really ask you for anything different. Then, too, I seem to just sort of slip into being inept or less adult when I'm around you. I sort of see you as the mom, so I think maybe I act like a kid who needs caretaking." Anna looked like a light bulb had just turned on in her head. She stated, "And when I see you act like a kid, I let it trigger all my caretaking behaviors." "You're right," Bob said enthusiastically. "It's not you or me; it's us." "Seems that's so," I added. "Anna's caretaking motherly behavior is triggered by your inept childlike behavior, Bob, and your inept childlike behavior is triggered by Anna's motherly caretaker actions. That's your cycle. Now, how are you two going to help each other to do something else? It's not enough to know what's wrong. You have to know and practice doing something different to change it."

Anna and Bob were bright; they caught on faster than many people do. Nonetheless, it still took some hard work and a lot of new learning to change their codependent cycle into love-filled CoRecovery.

For couples the term codependent suggests two people locked in a destructive cycle in which both are dependent on each other, or at least one is dependent on the other, as opposed to a healthy cycle, in which both are self-dependent. Anna and Bob had been trapped in just such a downward, destructive cycle.

WHAT CODEPENDENCY IS AND IS NOT

You may have already discovered that, so far, definitions of codependency vary widely. That's because codependency is a rather new discovery and a lot of different kinds of definitions are being attempted. There is, of course, more than one way to define something. For this word "codependency" I have read descriptive, psychological, clinical, behavioral, pathological, psychodynamic, symptomatic process, mathematical, logical, baffling ontological, epistemological, picayune, confused, fanciful, comic and stupid definitions. How mind-boggling this must be for the average person trying to figure out if this word really applies to them or their loved ones. Most of the definitions do overlap and share certain common elements. From them we can derive a specific understanding of this syndrome called codependency, which afflicts and destroys so many couples.

A major effort to reduce the confusion about defining codependency was made at the first National Conference on Codependency. At that time codependence was formally defined as "a pattern of painful dependence on compulsive behaviors and on approval from others in an attempt to find safety, self worth and identity" (Laign 1989). Soon this definition received strong criticism for its many evident shortcomings. Mostly this definition has been judged too broad, unclear, nonspecific, and it admits too many of the common behavior patterns that are generally considered typical of codependency (Hogg and Frank, 1992). Work continues to more accurately define this complex phenomenon. Perhaps the next national conference or the first international conference on codependency will make some improvements. Meanwhile, we know more than enough about the major characteristics and dynamics of codependency to successfully understand and constructively deal with it.

Codependency Concerns Couples

First, to understand codependency, let's look at a systemic or systems description. We'll apply this description to couples, instead of, as many people do, to individuals. I find most couples understand codependency quicker, and more accurately and practically this way. It gets us back closer to the original meaning of the word. When first used, codependent referred only to the spouse of a substance dependent person who was also a contributing part of their mate's overall addiction system. A typical example was the wife who kept bringing her alcoholic husband whiskey. She would do this because, in their relationship system, she couldn't stand to see the agony he purposely showed when doing without. She couldn't bear his displeasure when he wanted alcohol, which he of course used to manipulate her. Furthermore, she secretly feared he'd leave her if he ever got straight. That, of course, was because they both lived in a system in which healthy self-love and its subsequent sense of being adequate and okay could not grow. She believed she didn't really have what it took to hold him. Often this codependent system ended only when the alcoholic died of a drinking related cause, beat her to death in an alcoholic rage, or she suicided. The survivor carried this system of relating with them, found another person surprisingly similar to their former mate, and started the destructive codependent system over again. This repeating factor lead to the clinical finding that millions of couples were suffering from very similar dynamics even though substance addiction was often not a part of the picture.

The Problems Codependency Supports. At our counseling center, we often work in the area of medical psychotherapy. It was there we discovered that couples relating codependently sometimes keep a physical illness alive psychosomatically and block a cure or effective treatment. "So long as she's sick, I know she won't leave me," said one husband. His wife confessed, "So long as I'm sick, I know he'll show me kindness and attention." Both were enmeshed in a codependent cycle revolving around her illness.

We have also found a wide range of sex problems being supported and extended by codependent relationship systems. "Our relationship is organized around my husband's rescuing me from my affairs with users and losers. It's the only way we know," said one wife in a CoRecovery Group.

Money is said to be one of the most common problem couples have. At our counseling center, codependent relationships are often found in couples having repeated financial crises, couples stuck in both under- and overachiever patterns, workaholism, gambling addiction, and the stress of living beyond their means.

Of course the most common codependency problem involves couples simply stuck in unhappy and gradually worsening relationships. Often these relationships deteriorate into breakup or divorce that could have been avoided. Frequently one mate blames the other or themselves or outside influences, but remains blind to the mutually codependent system that destroys their relationship. Seldom do they see that the breakup was something they both caused through a subconscious teamwork of dependency. Both formed a dependency on one another and on a life-style that blocked their growth and promoted only the deterioration of their loving.

A Couples Definition of Codependency. From these examples of couples in dysfunction we can derive a broad couples- and systems-oriented definition of codependency. *Codependency means being partners for love in a relationship afflicted by destructive dependencies. These dependencies inhibit the growth of mutual healthy self-love and mate-love, and the maintenance of a healthy love-filled system of relating.* The good news is that the power of healthful love can reverse the whole downward cycle of codependent couples.

In regard to "individual's" codependency means a tendency or compulsion to get and stay in such relationships until either the relationship, or one or both of the individuals, is seriously harmed or destroyed. Death by addiction, suicide, couples violence or psychologically fomented illness is the eventual outcome of unchecked codependency in both individuals and couples. In couples and families it leads to needless breakups, children programmed to be codependent, endless wasted hours spent in various states of emotional agony, greatly reduced productivity, and the agonies of love-starved living.

Codependency and The Addicted

Codependency was identified when it was discovered that many alcoholics had spouses who were addictively dependent on their relationship to the addict. Upon losing one alcoholic spouse, many would marry another and even a third or fourth. Sadly a large number had suicidal breakdowns, were killed or involved in alcoholic violence, developed serious stress illnesses or became chemical addicts themselves. Since the original discovery of codependency, clinical research has found it exists in many relationships which do not involve chemical dependency. The outcomes, however, if unchecked, can eventually be just as serious.

Codependency can be described as being compulsively dependent for love on a dependent person who is in turn unable to love healthfully or consistently. The inconsistency of love returned is itself behaviorally addictive. It works much like a gambling addiction. Codependents never know if their efforts at love will meet with love returned, with punishment or with indifference. This intermittent reinforcement of their efforts is highly addictive. Thus many people define codependency as a behavior addiction.

Addictions help people grow increasingly dependent and rob them of healthful self-dependency. This is often the case with codependency. In couples work, I like to use the term, self-dependency, instead of independence, because independence has the emotional connotation of apart from and alone, which is not at all what a couple's remedy for codependency is all about.

Self-Perpetuating Codependency

Codependency can operate as a self-perpetuating system in two people's interactions. With less than a systems understanding, many of the most important elements are left out.

A more detailed couples system definition goes like this: *Codependency is occurring in a relationship when both partners act in a destructive interactive pattern which maintains and increases addictive-like psychological dependency and decreases the growth and maintenance of healthful self-dependence.*

Let's look at a typical case that demonstrates this type of codependency interaction system.

> Carol started taking over the handling of Dwane's finances ostensibly because he was so busy. Dwane gradually became dependent on her for this. As he did so, he grew to expect it. When she told

him he probably couldn't afford certain things, he became angry, blaming her for mismanagement and inaccuracy. She became afraid of his anger and told him less and less about his financial affairs. When he discovered a disagreeable financial fact, he'd fly into a rage. This in turn increased her fear and tension so she hid even more from him. To get his approval she began to lie, painting his economic picture as more rosy than it really was. She started making small and unusual mistakes. When he discovered one, they fought. She increasingly became a perfectionist, fearfully checking and rechecking her figures. This meant that things didn't get done on time. Seeing this, he grew even more disrespectful, critical and domineering. Soon their sex life suffered; they were no longer affectionate to each other. Their whole relationship was being destroyed. Three times they broke up, couldn't stand to be apart, reunited and within a month were at it again.

Then they heard about our center's CoRecovery couples program and tentatively entered CoRecovery counseling. Both quickly discovered they had grown up in love-stingy homes that led each of them to be insecure. Dwane saw that his insecurity and his father's modeling helped him become dependent on power tactics and critical domination. He also saw that Carol seemed to try harder every time he got mad and that reinforced his tendency to get angry with her. It helped his insecure self feel powerful and important.

Carol discovered and admitted that at first she liked Dwane's powerful domination. For the first time in her life someone was paying attention to her. It helped her feel important and was far better than the indifference she had experienced at home.

Dwane's critical anger was also a powerful sexual turn-on at first. In the early days of the cycle they built together, Carol would be sure she got caught at some little mistake. After his anger she would get seductive and they would have very intense sex together. However, later Dwane's criticism wore away her self-esteem and became a sexual turn-off. Later Carol admitted some of her unusual mistakes were secretly made to get back at him for his rages. Revenge gave her a secret glee even though she knew he would be angry. Carol discovered what she really wanted most from Dwane was approval, thankfulness and signs showing he valued her. That's why she had begun to take over his finances in the first place.

Carol and Dwane discovered one of codependency's great, tragic truths. What they had been doing to make it better had been making it worse. Even knowing how their downward spiral worked did little to stop this cycle of destruction. That's because so far they didn't know what to do instead. A second great, tragic truth about codependency is that until you know what to do differently, you keep interacting codependently even though you know it's wrong. All the knowledge in the world about what's codependent doesn't show a couple what to do in its place.

Carol and Dwane both realized they had only immature and inadequate ideas about how to show each other love. This was their greatest failing. They felt they loved each other but how to give that love to each other was a total mystery. Love-stingy homes, totally dysfunctional ideas garnered from fairy tales, TV, movies and novels, churches that taught more against sex than about love, schools that ignored the subject and a society that sent warped messages at best had all prepared them to fail at giving and receiving love. Now to survive as a couple they would have to find a way to learn the interactions of love.

In their CoRecovery group Carol and Dwane both saw how couples were constructing an upward spiral of love interactions by learning and practicing the eight major classes of love-demonstrating behavior, which you will learn in this book. Slowly, like those other couples, they began to replace codependency interactions with healthy love behaviors. It was arduous and they often slipped back, but it worked and they learned the teamwork required to make healthy love grow in place of codependency. Increasingly by combining their insights and perceptions they unraveled the intricacies of their particular system of codependency. They learned to replace codependency interactions with love interactions. As they progressed Carol and Dwane became successful as a couple.

What Codependency Is Not

If you read some other writings on codependency or have been to certain codependency workshops you may have been led to believe codependency includes every known human problem. One of my neophyte trainee therapists enthusiastically proclaimed, "Codependency explains everything!" Wrong, no, sorry. Accurately used, codependency usefully explains more than a lot of psychological concepts but it doesn't even touch the vast majority of human behavior.

Unfortunately you can find lists of so-called signs or symptoms of codependency which include a great many things that can be caused by something other than codependency. It's true that codependence in some people may cause certain kinds of sex problems, energy depletion, sleepiness, underproductivity, a sense of inadequacy, feelings of worthlessness, anxiety, depression, denial behaviors, dependency, withdrawal and compulsive coping. However, diabetes can also produce these symptoms. So can a fair number of other diseases and a host of other mental and emotional conditions.

Unhappily, whenever a psychological malady is newly identified, a lot of people are diagnosed as having it who don't. Codependency has become something of a fad diagnosis and that often means a misdiagnosis. This type of fad diagnosis often leads to misdirected treatment and a counter fad to discredit the original concept and the terms that define it. This has already begun with codependency. There are people who would have been more appropriately treated with other approaches. There are also people who, because of this and other mistakes being made with the concept of codependence, say that the whole idea of codependence is wrong, or so frequently misused as to be useless.

There are many thousands more who affirm that codependency treatment rescued their lives and their sanity, if not their relationships. Relationships have been lost because the relationship itself was not in a CoRecovery form of treatment or counseling. Only when the couple is treated interacting with each other can their way of interacting be dealt with directly and thereby effectively improved. Sadly, many codependency programs never directly dealt with a couple's interactions and many relationships that might have been saved were lost.

One of the simplest definitions of codependency for couples is interacting as partners in destructive dependency. The codependent problems of couples occur primarily in the interactions. Unless the action and reaction patterns that make up interactions are dealt with directly, a couple's codependency, in turn, is not being directly addressed. Both partners may come to their relationship with predispositions to live codependently. When they start to actively relate the real codependency of a couple can be seen, understood and directly improved. Unless the interactions improve, the couple doesn't improve.

Now let's look at what may be the most common way codependency is misconstrued.

> I stopped going to my CoDa (Codependency Anonymous) group when I got criticized for handing someone my handkerchief when they were crying. I was told that I was exhibiting codependent behavior. The week before a woman brought cookies and she was told that was very codependent behavior. Is it?

These statements show how codependency can be misunderstood and misrepresented. Some have thought that any favor done for another, any good deed that helps someone, every gesture of good will toward the unfortunate, the suffering, especially for anyone in trouble, is symptomatic of someone who has the codependent problem of trying to compulsively fix someone in order to feel okay themselves. This kind of narrow dogmatic thinking that one behavior represents enough evidence to diagnose someone is both ridiculous and destructive.

Let's get very clear on this. Knowing one behavior that someone does tells us absolutely nothing conclusive about anyone. It takes dozens, sometimes even hundreds, of behaviors following in a pattern before we can even sensibly suspect some kind of factor or trend may exist in a personality. This then has to be checked out many ways before we can be sure. No one behavior can tell you if someone is suffering from codependency, or anything else for that matter.

Acts of kindness and help, even actions that rescue people who don't need rescuing, can have many motivations other than codependent ones. Simple habits, childhood training to be considerate, uncomplicated care, empathy, love of fellow humans and innate tendencies to nurture can and do exist without being contaminated with codependency. On the less positive side, acting to assist or take care of someone can be a conscious manipulation, or con, an act designed to get religious credit, "brownie points with God," a duty, a penitence or one-upmanship.

It is true that in a codependent couple, one or both partners may exhibit a lot of caretaking, curative safeguarding, and fixing behaviors. However, that does not mean all such behaviors are symptoms of codependency and are therefore sick. The truth is altruistic behaviors do exist and they often do both the giver and the receiver a lot of good. If anyone doubts this, they have only to look at the experiments of the renowned stress-reduction specialist Dr. Hans Selye (1976). From his research he concluded that people who enjoyed their altruistic behavior definitely lived longer and had less illness than did comparison groups without such altruism.

Codependency . . . 2

So Just How Codependent Is Our Relationship?

No couple will exhibit all the traits of codependency. Every couple has its special configuration of symptoms. To help you see if your relationship is afflicted by the destructive symptom known as codependency, here are some things to look for. I call these *the seven core symptoms of couples codependency.*

Caretaking Instead of a Love-Sharing

In the simplest codependence systems, one mate is most frequently in the caretaker, fixer, rescuer, controller or safeguarding role. That mate tries to be a superparent, working hard to make sure their mate is okay. That is how they can occasionally feel something-like okay in their relationship. Naturally, the partner often facilitates this caretaker role by repeatedly getting in jams, needing rescuing, fixing, or safeguarding, something like a troublesome child does. The caretaker takes responsibility for the feelings, well-being, choices, wants, needs, sometimes even thoughts, and the partner lets them. The caretakers, of course, get to dodge being responsible for their feelings because they are so busy taking care of their mates. Thus, both have formed a partnership in which no one is self-dependent. Because of this, their own development stagnates and stagnation leads to deterioration, individually and as a couple.

A love-sharing couple's behaviors only occasionally involve caretaking. Instead they interact to help each other enjoy the world and to grow their self-dependent abilities. In love sharing, a mate may root for their spouse to succeed, but will not automatically take care of their mate's difficulties.

Right this minute, somewhere, there is a codependent couple in which one of them is for the hundredth time bailing the other out of one jam or another. Also, at this minute, there is a couple who has learned better teamwork; neither of them needs rescuing very often. Their time is spent sharing love, work and play. When facing a problem, the codependent spouses are sacrificing their own happiness for their mates', while their mates hope for, count on, expect or demand that sacrifice. The love-sharing couple is figuring out an "I win, you win" solution in which no one has to give up too much. When a codependent couple has not shown each other much love, they usually create a crisis so love can be shown through a rescuer or emergency caretaking effort.

The love-sharing couple is good both at loving themselves and at simply asking for love when they want it. "I would like a hug" is a typical statement by a love-sharing couple. "You never show me love when I need it" followed by tears or a fight is more typical of codependent relationships. By the way, a love-sharing couple's behavior will become clearer when you have read the chapters on the eight major ways humans have found to show each other love. Codependent couples who are infected or dominated by caretaking actions should be understood first.

Naturally caretaking systems can be more complicated than the example described above. Both parties may trade caretaker and caretakee roles. Sometimes codependent couples battle over who is to be the rescued or the rescuer. Various other complicated patterns involve more than just caretaker and caretakee, such as alternating between rescuer and victim and persecutor roles. In codependency, caretaking systems exist, grow and replace love-sharing behavior in all too many couples. CoRecovery from caretaking systems is often essential for a relationship to survive.

Blaming and Guilt Tripping Instead of Responsibility Taking and Sharing

Commonly, in codependency each partner blames the other for the bad feelings they have, for the situations they are in that they do not like, for not treating them the way they want to be treated, even for their life. Sometimes the blaming is secret; sometimes it happens in shouting matches. There are thoughts or statements like, "You make me feel. . . .," "If it were not for you. . . . You made me." The word "You," followed by negative blame dominates their speech.

A corollary to this is not taking responsibility for one's feelings and actions. Confronted by a problem, healthy couples tend to say "I," "we" and "us" a lot more than "You." "You" is reserved for words of affirmation, love, appreciation, enjoyment, and so on.

Often mixed with, preceding or following the blaming of each other come self-blame and feeling guilty, ashamed and generally down on oneself. There is no realization that they are probably only half of what went wrong. It is a joint pattern, much like a dance both partners engage in together.

So Just How Codependent Is Our Relationship?

In many complicated ways codependent partners try to influence each other by saying things designed to help the other feel guilty or ashamed. They were treated the same way growing up. Usually, it is all they know to do when something is not the way they want it. When they learn and habituate love-centered behaviors instead, they do much better.

It is important to know that blaming, shaming and laying guilt trips on others are the opposite of taking and sharing responsibility. Look at the difference this way:

Blaming leads us to say, "Look at what you did." Responsibility leads us to say, "Let's look at what can be done about this." Shaming sends a message that says, "Feel inadequate and inferior about yourself." Responsibility-based talk sends a message, "You are what the word means, 'response-able,' and therefore, able to make competent responses." "You cannot do anything right" is a lot different than, "You can fix that" or "Try that again" and "We all get better with practice." Guilt messages say you are at fault, bad, sinful and must suffer. This helps people de-energize with depression or waste their energy with defensiveness. True responsibility taking points to doing something about whatever the problem is and therefore getting one's energy focused on positive actions. Statements like "Let's try to grow past this" come to replace "You are really bad, you sinner, you slut, you bastard," and all the looks and sounds people make to trigger their mate's guilt.

Interactions That Work Against the Growth of Healthy Self-Love

A good healthy relationship helps people grow their self-esteem, self-confidence, sense of self-worth and self-reliance, all parts of the larger category of healthful self-love. Codependency and dependencies in general work to block self-development. Contrast: "Sure, Honey, I am all for your going to school. It will be good for you and that will be good for us. Let's see how we can make it work," with, "How could you be so selfish as to want to go to school and leave me and the kids alone all that time? How could you neglect your duties like that? Something must be really wrong with you."

In healthy love couples, both work at helping each other feel better about themselves. In codependency, one or both use put-downs. Sometimes one or both are putting down the same person. Comments like, "You're so stupid" get replies like, "I'm sorry, you are right. I don't know how I can be so dumb." In this situation, both partners think one of them has to sacrifice self-approval for mate-approval so they can stay together. They do not realize that whatever diminishes one member of a team diminishes the team as a whole and conversely, whatever helps a team member improve, improves the team. Healthy couples are a co-equal team against problems. Codependent couples are a team divided against itself. In a negative sense, they are unknowingly cooperating with their problems.

Sometimes one spouse gets a lot of praise from the other but it is usually not quite real praise. Playing up to, praising to placate, and compliments to gain approval or some advantage are not really praise. In healthy couples, the praise is a free gift. There is a balance of praise going back and forth between both mates.

Many codependent couples cooperate to repress the discovery and development of what is best in each of them. They fear discovering what is really there. For safety's sake, they promote the stagnation of sameness and seldom change. Generally, they live by being afraid of what their true feelings may be and therefore much is left unsaid. What knowledge they do have of each other's inner selves grows stale and out-of-date as they play out the same old roles, say the same old things and even have the same old fights and crises.

In the healthy couple, there is cooperation in exploring the new, the different and the best that both can become. Love is pro-growth. Fear is anti-growth. The codependent couple so often lets fear, and consequently safety seeking, be more important than love. The couple that allows or makes love be the more important thing takes little, and sometimes even big, risks for the growth of each and their relationship. Fear does not dominate—love does. That means growth occurs, not stagnation with its subsequent deterioration and destruction.

Sometimes low self-love is masked or hidden behind a mask of egotism, arrogance or grandiosity. In these false forms of self-love, there is an underlying message, "I am worthy and you are not." In healthy self-love, no one has to be put-down or seen as less. Therefore, little focus or effort goes to proving "I" or "we" are better. Status symbols do not matter much and one upmanship is unappealing to the healthy couple. As one couple who used to strive to impress said it, "Now we know we're good, so now we can finally afford to look cheap." That is real comfort.

Enmeshed Boundaries Instead of Clear and Honored Individuality

Codependence blurs the boundaries between mates. "I don't know where my limits are," said one wife. "I don't know when I'm doing too much or too little," "When to ask for more," "Whether or not I'm wanting the impossible." These comments are common in many codependent relationships. It is not unusual for one spouse at one time to say they will not tolerate something from their mate and then to ask that mate to tolerate the same type of behavior. "No, I won't let you have a night out with the boys and by the way, is it okay if I spend the evening with my friends?" is the kind of double standard permission giving that goes on in some codependent couples. Who is in charge of whom? "Am I in charge of me or are you?" "Are you my boss or am I?" "Is anybody in charge?" "Do I let you run my life?" "Should I be running yours?" These are the confused attitudes of many couples.

In this system spouses do not know when they have crossed over their partner's boundary and their mate feels violated, hurt, set up, invaded, betrayed, inconsiderately dealt with, and sent double messages. I remember one man saying, "Never even touch my tool box" and a week later, "Oh, whenever you need a hammer or screwdriver, just look in my tool box."

In one of our CoRecovery couples groups a woman advised all the other females in the group to "always let your man have you sexually whenever he wants you." When her mate said, "I want you tonight," she blurted out, "Can't you see I'm already too tired?" Amazingly, it was not until she got some feedback that she could realize she had just sent very conflicting messages.

There is a process in human development called individuation. It has to do with the processes of psychologically becoming an individual. When we are too enmeshed with others, we do not know when we must say "no" for our own good. Therefore, we can, without knowing it, teach our mates to abuse us. One wife in a couples group said, "I got so angry doing all the housework and him never lifting a hand after I started a full-time job. Then I realized I never told him, 'Now it's too much for me and I want some help.' I kept doing it all and telling him I didn't mind doing it all and getting so angry at him for believing me. Finally, in desperation, I asked him for help and he pitched right in. Then I saw it. I had expected him to read my mind. I did not really understand loving him doesn't mean he's inside my brain. I'm still an individual. We're not really one person; we're two, and I have to set my limits. I have to tell him what they are."

Healthy love-centered couples help each other to be individuals with distinct differences and limits. Their boundaries are recognized and honored. Boundary disputes are democratically dealt with by coequals. "She's a night person and I'm a morning person," one man laughingly said. "And we're just fine with that," his wife added. A new couple in their CoRecovery group expressed surprise. She said, "I don't see how you do it. I feel hurt and rejected every time my husband doesn't go to bed when I do." Her husband then slowly added, "I've been harboring resentment for ages because I thought she should get up with me in the morning. I guess love doesn't mean we're the same after all."

Tolerational love, which you will learn about later in this book, is a key ingredient couples use to work out their boundary problems. Healthy self-love insists people discover and set their own boundaries. This in turn helps a person take responsibility for his thoughts, feelings, and actions. It also helps one stop taking responsibility for others. Boundary setting limits the tendency to undemocratically manipulate and control our mates. It also diminishes feeling hurt and blaming our spouses. Boundary problems are intertwined with another major area of difficulty for codependent couples' control.

Sharing Contention and Chaos, Instead of Democratic Control

One of the many wonderful things to see in couples counseling is how codependent couples create a democratic control over their lives. It is hard work and usually very confusing at first, but the results are outstanding. Often the couple operates with one of them trying to control everything except themselves. Their partner may relinquish control or try to rebel, escape, or take over. Sometimes they alternate in these behaviors.

In childhood, we do not control our lives. Events conspire to overwhelm us and bring us hurt, fear, confusion, sorrow and feelings of inadequacy. To save ourselves and our loved ones from reexperiencing these feelings and events, we sometimes try to control others and events that are simply beyond our control. If we had particularly difficult experiences growing up, our control issues may loom very large. Added to this, our culture teaches a man that, if he is going to be a real man, he has to be in charge, wear the pants in the family, be the all-knowing provider and protector, and generally operate like a dictator. Women on the other hand, are socially programmed to be "supermother," the perfect caretaker making sure everyone is always safe and happy. The dilemma for supermoms is how to control everyone's safety and happiness without being seen as controlling. The way to do this is through manipulation.

Manipulation requires secrecy, deceit, withholding information and an awful lot of work, since it is so indirect. Both males and females who grow up in dysfunctional families, where things can go suddenly and drastically wrong, are especially prone to manipulate. This is because it was the only way for them to stay safe.

Naturally, if we add addictions to the life of the couple, everything increasingly goes out of control. This, in turn, creates a growing anxiety about getting things under control. The pressure of that can be temporarily alleviated by the addiction, but the downward spiral is accentuated. Codependent couples commonly get into battles for control.

Communication methods often involve dogmatic opinions, coercion, begging, lying, bribing, threatening, blaming, and excessive advice. They can also include telling the other how they should and should not be, act, think and feel, intimidation, purposeful hurt, pouting, uncomfortable silences, and generally just about every communication error that can harm a long-term relationship. All of these methods are aimed at some short-term gain, and the long term is not recognized.

In CoRecovery groups couples see and learn to replace all these with love-centered democratic sharing. Negotiating and synthesizing their differing viewpoints, wants and ways, is at first a struggle. Later it becomes a chore, and finally a delight. Self-disclosure love is important to this process, but for most people it is very scary at first. "I feel so nude and vulnerable telling you what I really think and want, but I am starting to trust the way you deal with me." That is the cautious statement heard at this stage of things. Frustration, anger and disappointment are reduced when a couple adopts democratic, adult ways of controlling their life-style. Contention, consternation, and chaos lessen.

Interacting to Regulate Dependencies of All Sorts

The wife who buys her alcoholic husband beer acts to continue a dependency system. The husband will give her positive attention or negative attention, but at least some attention. "He needs me, what would he do without me, I'm important to him," can be her feelings, coupled with guilt and inadequacy for being stuck in such a system.

More subtle and complicated are the ways couples support each other's dependencies. Simply denying that there is a problem is one of the surest ways to keep a dependency-based relationship going. Of course, it can and often does let things go too far—then it can be too late. One of the sad parts of the work I do is seeing people who come too late for help to save their relationship. Along with substance addictions, denial can be the greatest enemy to survival.

Sometimes, it is only one mate who sees something is happening to directly or indirectly destroy their relationship. One spouse sees a serious health issue, and the other denies it, until there is a heart attack or a stroke. Many a mate has faced a funeral after not being able to successfully communicate that they saw an addiction problem developing. Sometimes someone sees that insufficient self-love leads to insecurity; and this gives rise to defenses like jealousy, possessiveness, isolation, and a host of other problems.

If one mate ignores the spouse's understanding, destruction can still occur. Healthy couples learn to use the views, insights and knowledge of both partners. They acknowledge that their spouse may have useful understandings, which they themselves lack. Codependent couples all too often let problems—that only one of them sees—eat away at the relationship until someone leaves, or someone dies.

It is so tragic to hear, "I knew we were not doing well, so I introduced her to cocaine to help us loosen up with each other, and make love better. Now she is dead of an overdose, and I am hooked." More subtle, but no less tragic are messages like, "Even after his heart attack, I kept feeling I would lose him to some other woman if he really trimmed down. I kept cooking and he kept eating. Now I know I helped him die way sooner than he should have." Equally sad are realizations like, "I never really believed my jealousy could run her off until it was too late," or " Now I see that to save himself, he had to escape what we were doing to each other," or "If I'd only done more sooner, I think we would still be together."

For other couples, it is a close call that still represents years of needless agony. "We almost didn't make it," "We nearly destroyed what we had," "I'm so glad we came for help in time because it was almost over," "God, we wasted so many years and we have so much to repair," are the statements of many couples in CoRecovery.

The most common destroyer of relationships, in my professional opinion, is not knowing how to show and receive love. Often the couple or one mate has a growing sense of this. Unfortunately they do not want to believe anything is wrong, so they keep doing little or nothing about it. Instead, they want to believe our culture's destructive lies about love and how it works. Our culture teaches incredibly ruinous things like when you are in love you will automatically "live happily ever after." In our conscious mind, we may have some idea that this is not true, but we so want to believe it anyway. Believing this myth is such a convenient cop-out, easier than going to all the trouble to learn what it takes to make a love relationship work.

"If I have to tell him, it somehow spoils it," is another superdestructive message our culture teaches about love. This message provides a great excuse for not doing the real work of learning to communicate ones' wants and needs. "If you really loved me, you'd know what I want" is an anticommunication, anticloseness and antilove way of thinking. Lamentably, it is common in the tangle of codependency. With it comes the ridiculous societal training that you do not have to know your own needs. Our culture teaches that it is your spouse's job to know and take care of your needs; if they really love you, they will magically do this. As adults, it is our job to discover our needs and communicate them to our mates. Without self-disclosure, our loved ones are greatly limited in what they can know about us, or do for us.

A similar way codependent couples help each other continue destructive dependencies is to avoid seeing their own personal realities.

"She's starting to exercise so I'd better work out too," "He votes Democrat, so I do too," "I guess I'm mad at Mom because she is. . . ." all show a loss of touch with one's unique reality. This inhibits the chance to integrate and grow from difference. People deny their perceptions, values, and join together as one, like our culture teaches. This leads to enmeshment. Enmeshment compounds your inability to distinguish your wants and needs. This, in turn, leads to not getting your needs met. Destructive codependency continues without confrontation.

Codependent couples must replace their patterns of stagnation with the ways of loving that produce growth. The eight major ways of loving accomplish this and will be introduced later.

Codependency Instead of Loving Others as You Love Yourself

In the ancient Torah, the third book of the library known as the Bible, Moses tells that God instructs us to love others as we love ourselves (Leviticus 19:18). Jesus used this as one of his two great commandments. Islam, Hinduism and Buddhism have very similar teachings. Notice, the admonition is to love others "as," not before or after, but "as" we love ourselves. This is precisely where many codependent relationships go wrong. Typically, in a codependent relationship, one or both partners are lousy at loving themselves, without the foggiest idea of how to do so. They are dependent on their mate to do that for them.

When you don't love yourself, it is very difficult to believe, trust or receive love from another. Love works much like a nurturing food. But in codependent relationships, there is love deprivation, hunger, malnutrition, and the killing force of love starvation. Codependency so often means needless and useless self-sacrifice. It also means avoidance of self-discovery, self-understanding and self-healing. A healthy relationship requires healthy self-love and self-development. In all my years of working with couples I have found that knowing how to love each other, and themselves at the same time, is the most important thing a couple can do to make a healthy relationship.

Codependency often means desperately seeking love, but being unable to accept the love when it comes. This, in turn leads to anxiety that we are not loved. Depression caused by love malnutrition is also common. Too little love in our lives leads to anger about the situation and extremism in our attempts to be loved. In this condition we commonly repeat all the things our family-of-origin did to get love, things that seldom worked. As this love hunger grows, we may rely on almost anything that gives us relief. These substitutes for love include addictive chemicals, superstitions, stupid cultural concepts about love, destructive game-playing, and even real and pretended illness to get attention. When all else fails, suicide can result.

"I didn't feel okay about us until I learned to love myself, while I was attempting to love my spouse," is the type of statement many couples in CoRecovery begin to make. "Now we can give and receive love simultaneously," is another comment couples make as their CoRecovery teamwork improves. "I kept trying to prove I was good enough for him to love, and it never seemed to work. Now, I have a sense of being so lovable, he'd be crazy not to love me," is how one ecstatic spouse put it.

A COUPLE'S CODEPENDENCY CHECKUP

Here is a short, beginner's screening exam to help you see if your love relationship is threatened by codependency problems. This is not a comprehensive test; it is only a screening device aimed at hitting the major, core issues that afflict couples. It works like this:

Using the understanding you have so far garnered from the discussion of the seven core symptoms of couples codependency, read and rate each of the following seven statements.

Taking the Checkup

If you believe a statement in no way describes your relationship, circle the word, "None."

If you think the statement has a little truth in its description of what goes on in your mated love life, circle the word, "Little."

If you think a statement represents more than a little truth about how you and your partner interact, circle the word, "Some."

If you see a largely true statement about your love relationship system, circle the word, "Much."

Be sure you and your mate rate these statements entirely independently. Do not try to influence, or be influenced by, your partner. Here are the seven statements:

1. Concerning Caretaking Versus Love Sharing:

I think our system of relating involves one or both of us being in a caretaker role too frequently, and interacting as coequal, love-sharing adults too infrequently.

None Little Some Much

So Just How Codependent Is Our Relationship?

2. Concerning Blame, Shame and Guilt Versus "Response Ability":

I see our relationship as having too many blaming, shaming, judging, condemning or guilt-oriented interactions and too few interactions where we both responsibly act as a team.

None Little Some Much

3. Concerning Healthy, Self-Love Development:

In my view, our interactions too often end up helping one, or both of us, to feel bad about ourselves, and too seldom helping us to grow healthy self-love.

None Little Some Much

4. Concerning Boundary Issues:

In my perception, one or both of us experiences too much confusion, pain, or conflict over boundary issues; we do not work enough as a team to help us both to be loving, well-differentiated individuals.

None Little Some Much

5. Concerning Relating Democratically:

Our way of relating is not sufficiently democratic; we do not lovingly share power and control over our life together.

None Little Some Much

6. Concerning Destructive Dependencies:

Our relationship system continues destructive dependencies in one or both of us, more than it helps us to become healthfully and cooperatively self-dependent.

None Little Some Much

7. Concerning Loving Ourselves as We Love Each Other:

Our system of relating does not sufficiently help us both to practice loving ourselves while we love each other and all too often one or both of us exists in a state of unhealthy love hunger.

None Little Some Much

Understanding Your Ratings

Rating everything with a "None" in all likelihood represents denial. Even the best of relationships will not honestly get a "None" on all seven statements. Five or six "None" ratings by either spouse, or ten or more by a couple, probably means there is a lot of denial of existing codependence.

If nothing gets rated as high as a "Some," denial is likely. Even very healthy relationships have at least one "Some" rating after being rated by both spouses.

If one or both partners rate everything or nearly everything with a "Much," extremism is the likely interpretation. Unfortunately, extremism is one of the commonly noted symptoms of advanced codependency.

Four to six "Little," one or two "Some," and possibly one "None" rating by both mates suggests a less-than-average amount of codependency. Unfortunately, our cultures' average amount of codependency is quite high.

Three to six "Much" ratings by either spouse strongly indicates something is severely wrong and professional help is definitely recommended.

Two or more "Much" ratings means professional help is still advisable, especially if things seem to be getting worse. A majority of "Some" ratings indicates the same thing.

An even scattering of "Little" and "Some" ratings suggests it would be best for both of you to do a lot of self-help actions to improve your relationship.

If both of you rate your interaction system with "Little" on most statements, and with just a few "Some" ratings, you could stand some self-help work, but in all likelihood, you are doing tolerably well, or better than average.

If one of you has given mostly "Some" and a few "Much" ratings, while the other has given mostly "Little" and "None" ratings, the gap between your perceptions is too large. You are safest trusting the perception of the one who gave the highest ratings. If you err on the side of minimization the problem is likely to get worse.

Now, this is only a beginner's screening device. The best thing to do is read the rest of this book, which will give you a much more complete understanding of codependency and relationships. Then I suggest you retake this little exam, and use these results to evaluate how your relationship is faring.

WHAT CAN WE DO ABOUT A CODEPENDENT RELATIONSHIP?

Lots! First, keep reading. Focus on all the knowledge about love and how it is successfully done. Experiment with new behaviors. Be kind to yourself and your mate about lapses, mistakes, awkward attempts. Like everything new we try, we rarely do it well at first. Never cop out with the negative game call, "Strike one, we are out." The couples who keep at it are the ones who win at it. We have lots of new and better knowledge about love, but like everything worthwhile, it takes work to win with that knowledge.

If your mate is not yet involved in learning what this book has to say, ask him or her to get started. Underlining or highlighting what you call most important and asking your mate to do the same in another color is a good way to use this book. Read each other's highlighted sections lovingly instead of fighting over them. If that is too hard, write each other letters using the book's concepts. This is how couples can get a lot of mileage out of this type of book. If your spouse is reluctant to work with you on all of this, I recommend extremely loving nagging. If things seem to be getting worse rapidly, I recommend help from a counselor trained in CoRecovery couples work, along with closely studying the information in this book. Joining several support groups, attending seminars, retreats and workshops on CoRecovery, couples' issues, and love, can all be very helpful. There will be more about just how to find these at the end of this book.

There are many good codependency counseling and therapy programs for individuals in counseling centers, clinics and treatment centers across the United States. They can also be found in Canada and many European countries, and are being developed in other parts of the world as well. For those whose experiences with codependency are devastatingly painful or severely debilitating, there are fine inpatient hospital treatment programs, often covered by medical insurance.

Some treatment programs include family therapy and that can help a lot. The most up-to-date treatment facilities have added special couples CoRecovery programs. These are the programs most likely to lead to the cure of the relationship as well as the cure of the individual. For some time now, research has been showing that both relapses and divorces are more likely when one spouse is treated without the inclusion of their mate in therapy (Olsen, Russell & Sprinkle 1980; Jackobson 1978; Gurmond and Kiniskern 1981; Byers, Cohen & Horshbarger 1979; Cookerly 1976;

Marlatt and Gordon 1980). If a full inpatient treatment is needed, it pays to ask about what special programs are available for *couples*.

Codependency can be intensely harmful. It makes sense to get professional help whenever your personal efforts do not seem to be enough. Fortunately, good help can be found. Remember, even though millions of couples have been destroyed by codependency, you do not have to belong to that group. Know that thousands of couples are learning to defeat the destructiveness of codependency. Together, they are learning about and developing healthy, successful, love relationships. I have seen truly awful couples use this knowledge and become truly wonderful. I have worked with incredibly destructive relationships and seen miracles occur. The worst of couples, when they work hard to learn and use love behaviors, reduce their destructiveness and increase their constructiveness. I am betting, if you need to do this, you can. So let's get on with learning about the things that really work for couples.

Codependency . . . 3

What Is a Love-Healthy Couple?

We all keep doing things that don't work, even when we know they don't work. We keep doing this until we learn what does work, and still it's a problem. This is supertrue in relationships. You see, we are indeed creatures of habit. We are also creatures of program. The part of our brain that works much like a computer contains programs that make us return again and again to ways of thinking, acting and feeling that simply do not work. Until we learn what does work, all we do is what we know to do. Even if we manage to stop a failing behavior all we know to do is "nothing." We must learn and repeatedly practice what does work until it pushes out the old programs and becomes part of our new self-programming. Even then an old program can be occasionally triggered, and we find ourselves doing things in old ways instead of new ways. Understanding all this is exceptionally important for love relationships. We must know what works before we can work it.

The problem with some codependency treatment and counseling efforts is that they do a good job of helping people know what's wrong, and what not to do. However they do a poor job helping people know what to do instead. Let's start looking at what really works in helping couples grow healthy, strong, close, intimate love.

OVERHAULING YOUR MIND'S MODEL OF WHAT WORKS

If you are like most people, in your head is a conglomerate of contradictory, immature, and unworkable ideas of how a couple's life together is supposed to look. Our models of life guide our actions. If our model is a mess, our life is a mess. Models are mostly subconscious, so a certain amount of consciousness-raising is in order.

Most of our ideas about how a couple's love is supposed to work are stuck in the year 1174. In that year the Countess de Champagne wrote the *Code of Love* stating such destructive things as:

> "If love lessens, it dies speedily and rarely regains health."
> "Suspicion and the jealousy it kindles increases love's worth."
> "The least presumption compels the lover to suspect evil of the co-lover" (Langdon-Davies 1927, 267).

These and many other of our culture's Dark Age ideas about romantic love describe false love rather than real love. Versions of these false love ideas are part of the subconscious model in many relationships. They may be destructively guiding you today.

A Sample of Society's Self-Defeating Old Programs

Let's contrast some of the more common elements of poor love models with what really works according to modern research.

Old Program 1: Love is Jealous.

Current Understanding: Jealousy is caused by a lack of self-love involving a subconscious insecurity. The subconscious process believes, "Since I don't love me, you can't either. Therefore you will leave me for someone better." Healthy self-love development is crucial for conquering pathological jealousy according to many authorities in the field (Clayton and Smith 1977). Our current understanding is in accordance with the even older teaching: "Love is not jealous" (I Corinthians 13:4).

Old Program 2: We will live happily ever after (automatically).

Current Understanding: The truth is relationships end, one way or another. We're usually in denial of this, but the fact remains that someone almost always dies first. If that doesn't happen, the relationship ends some other way, although the love itself may continue. If we get out of denial, we can use the truth that relationships end to enjoy them while they last. We can also be motivated to work on the quality of the relationship, and not take it for granted.

Old Program 3: Love is magic . . . therefore we don't have to work at it.

What is a Love-Healthy Couple?

Current Understanding: When you love there may be a component of feelings you can call magical. But success in love takes a lot of work, just like everything else worthwhile. Just ask any marriage counselor. Research shows that the marriages that work are the ones that are worked on (Ard 1969).

Old Program 4: "If he(she) really loved me he(she) would know what I want and how to show me love. If I have to ask it somehow spoils it."

Current Understanding: Research into how healthy relationships are carried out shows that people in the relationship consistently and clearly work at communicating what they want. Anything less is destructive and may represent manipulative game playing (Beavers 1977).

Old Program 5: All's fair in love and war.

Current Understanding: Healthful love motivates people toward positive, truthful, constructive behaviors for all concerned. Various forms of false love tend to have the opposite effect (Maslow 1970). Our current understanding is in accordance with the even older teaching: "Love does not rejoice at wrong but rejoices in the right." (I Corintheans 13:6), which means wrongs are not fair in love.

These five subconsciously programmed misconceptions are only a fraction of our society's cultural training which directs us toward hindered, harmed and destroyed love relationships. You may come from the kind of semifunctional or dysfunctional family background that strongly predisposes you toward codependent relationships. If so, you have a lot more reprogramming to do. The "how to do it wrong" training is compounded by society's misconceptions about love. Your family's failure training can be sorted out from what they did right. Remember, no parent or family was perfectly wrong about everything. Fortunately we now have a lot of counselors, therapists, workshops, and self-help books to accomplish this sorting. Even more helpful is learning what to do that works. So, here is a beginner's guide to what a successfully functioning couple might look like contrasted with a codependent, dysfunctional couple.

HOW HEALTHY LOVE DIFFERS FROM CODEPENDENCY

Self- and Other-Love

Loving another as you love yourself is well practiced in healthy relationships. In codependency we do one of the following: (a) Either one or both of us acts to love ourselves only after we've sacrificially or parentally acted to love the other; (b) In frustration one or both of us has given up on loving the other, and now is mostly acting only to love ourselves; or (c) One of us is mostly a taker of the other's love action, giving little in return.

Here is an example. If I sacrificially give you a back rub when I'm tired, it can be an okay back rub but I'm less when it's over, even though you may be more. However, if I give you a back rub more selfishly, enjoying your oohs and ahhs, the sensual feeling of your skin, and the specialness of our connection, we both come out ahead. This loving yourself while doing acts to love another can be achieved more often than people realize. That leads us to the next point.

Giving and Receiving Love

Healthy, loving couples in good teamwork give and receive love in the eight major ways that love can be given and received. In codependent relationships love is given in only a few of those ways. When love is demonstrated, it's often poorly received at best. The teamwork of giving and receiving love, mutually and simultaneously, is often sabotaged by codependency-based actions. Frequently a crisis is precipitated before both people even get close to showing and receiving love simultaneously. As one client put it, "I knew you really loved me every time you bailed me out of jail; so I kept getting drunk and thrown into jail, when I needed to know you loved me. When you stopped bailing me out, I thought you had stopped loving me, and were only loving yourself. I didn't know you could do both at the same time."

Tragically a significant subgroup of codependent couples believes that all their love needs should be taken care of by their mate. They are not supposed to be self-loving or to get love from friends and family. When they learn and make habits of the eight major ways of showing and receiving love, whole new worlds of healthy, happiness open up to them. All eight ways and how to learn them are presented in Chapters Five, Six and Seven.

The inability to give and receive love simultaneously leads both partners to be love hungry, love malnourished and eventually love starved.

Love deprivation works just like food deprivation. In both food and love hunger there is irritability and aggravation. In both food and love malnutrition there is low energy, growing depression, and anxiety. In both food and love starvation there is major breakdown; physical and psychological malfunctioning ensues, and there is increased susceptibility to illness and the growing likelihood of death. A good diet of love works the opposite because love nourishes; it improves the immune mechanisms, strengthens, and energizes, much like a good food diet does. In the discussion of the eight major ways to demonstrate love we will cover some of these physical health effects.

Democratic Interdependent Love

In healthy loving couples there is a democratic interdependent cooperation. This includes considerable two-way pleasure and a problem-solving orientation. The outcome of democratic discussions and disputes is often a synthesis of wants.

In codependent couples control efforts are much more common. These control efforts result in covert or overt rebellion, interspersed with periods of submission. Seldom are both partner's wants synthesized. When codependent couples start to learn democratic, loving communication systems, they often experience anxiety and confusion. The anxiety is a vague fear that they are giving up whatever control they thought they had. The confusion is in trying to understand something so foreign as relationship democracy. When they learn and practice democratic loving they reap the benefits. A sense of closeness and adequacy develops. Many people suffering from codependent problems feel a big sense of inadequacy because all their efforts at control eventually fail. The simple truth is we really can't control others, but we can cooperate. People suffering from codependency may intellectually understand this but they have a hard time understanding it at the heart and gut level. Cooperation does not mean one of us must surrender.

One client summed it up when he said, "I'll never forget how we got bent out of shape over which way to discipline the kids. Now it's almost automatic. We use a combination of both our ways. But, damn, it took a lot to learn how to do that."

Codependent mates often try to control their relationships. Their sense of self-worth is connected to the outcome of that control. If the outcome is good their sense of self-worth temporarily rises. If the outcome is bad their sense of self-worth plummets. Typical thinking is, "If I don't save him from himself, I'm not of any value." Affirmational love (Chapter Five) applied to yourself will help to solve this problem.

In healthy love relationships both people retain their sense of self-worth. Interdependence means a couple balances the load they jointly carry. "I'll pay the rent if you'll take care of the car, utilities, and appliance payments," "If you'll pick up the kids, I'll get the cleaning," "Let's alternate taking out the trash since neither of us likes to do it," and "I believe it's your turn to pick a movie," are typical statements made in an easygoing, practical but loving manner in interdependent relationships. We both lovingly depend on each other to do a lot. When someone doesn't get their part done, it's lovingly and democratically discussed. There is no punishment, guilt tripping, or withdrawal of love; no one has to feel love-deficient.

In codependency both mates commonly feel love-deficient when someone doesn't do their part. Typical codependency thinking is, "If I were a better person, I'd have taken care of that," or "I must not be important enough to my mate because if I were, he (or she) would have done that." "I'll have to try harder. I'm just not good enough." From this thinking flow actions of low self-worth and little confidence in a mate's love. Many spouses encountering these self-devaluing actions join in the devaluing process. One spouse who was working hard to come out of codependency said, "So long as I knew you felt bad about yourself I knew you wouldn't leave me. Every time I heard you beating up on yourself, I did too. It was my secret way to keep you around. I hid my insecurity in arrogance and phony, macho self-confidence to keep you down. Deep inside I felt I wasn't worth much, so I had to keep you feeling worse than me to keep from losing you."

This of course represents a very common kind of codependent relationship. One mate is overtly codependent and the other is covertly or secretly codependent. Neither of them feels the self-esteem that comes from healthy self-love. Their relationship is saturated with trying to fill the voids they feel, trying to stay safe, and trying to control what's going on. All this crowds out feeling or acting with love effectively, toward themselves or each other.

In healthy love couples act to support each other's self-love, not tear it down. "I really like seeing you proud of what you're accomplishing," "Strut your stuff, Baby," and "Self-confidence really looks good on you," typify the statements sent back and forth in healthy, loving couples. This, of course, greatly supports a couple's team spirit for interdependent cooperation. It can also be mutually pleasurable and contribute to joint problem solving.

When things go wrong in the life of a healthfully loving couple, self-love (and its components, self-esteem, self-confidence and self-reliance) doesn't suffer greatly. With codependence, self-love often decreases when the partner's feelings fall. "If my partner feels bad, I'm at fault," "I've failed if my partner fails," "I'm responsible for their feelings," are typical codependent relationship attitudes and thinking. I should make him (or her) happy and he (or she) should make me happy is a prevailing philosophy in codependency. On the other hand, a democratic love relationship is exemplified by these words: "I may help or assist my spouse toward happiness. I can share happiness with my mate. However, we don't control each other's happiness and we don't cause or make each other unhappy either. We are each in charge of our personal happiness. We are both the primary cause of our happiness and unhappiness. We may or may not let our mates help us with our emotional states and that's entirely up to us individually. My emotions are my responsibility, not my mate's. My mate's emotions are not my responsibility. I can offer sharing, I can care, and I can accept the same from my mate. I cannot fix, cure, create, cause, regulate, govern, manage, or direct my loved one's feelings. I can only assist with my input if my mate allows it. Whether my mate makes use of my input is up to my mate, not me. We can offer each other our thoughts, feelings, and assistance, but we cannot make each other adopt these. We are both independent people relating to each other, not enmeshed controllers of each other's life. With this understanding, we see we must interdependently relate democratically with love, because neither of us will ever control the other."

Truth Accepting and Truth Rejoicing

Codenial is characteristic of a host of relationships afflicted with codependency. Couples in healthy relationships jointly search for the truth. They also understand that both partners will have their independent view of the truth. They realize truth is seldom easily known. Truth may be stable but our knowledge of it is not. Therefore, healthy couples accept the ever-changing perceptions of truth. In codependency-filled relationships conspiring to dodge the truth is one of several common patterns. Interestingly, denial of both unpleasant and pleasant truths occurs.

One client reported, "When my brother told us we were suffering from codependency, just like he and his wife had, my first reaction was anger. And I denied it vehemently. My wife immediately chimed in with, 'That's about other people, not us.' Then I remember making the ridiculous statement that we absolutely were not codependent and at the same time asking what does that damn word mean anyway. We were denying something we knew nothing about. Later we learned how this teamwork in denial could be turned into teamwork for discovering truth."

A similar pattern involves one mate dogmatically pronouncing the truth, and the other mate being in a more passive "Yes, dear, of course you're right," compliant stance. Secretly the compliant spouse may have doubts. I remember the interaction of one couple's first visit in my office that went like this: Husband, "We don't drink too much." Wife, "What about your six-pack every night? Remember last Sunday morning's hangover, Honey?" Husband, "Oh darling, you know beer doesn't count, and we only get blasted once or twice a month on weekends." Wife, "How silly of me. You're right." Later, both were able to see they were too fearful to relate to each other without alcohol. Whenever one of them dodged the truth, the other quickly followed.

Blaming is one of the cleverest ways to deny the truth because it seems like you are trying to deal with it. Playing destructive blame games is common. Here are several ways the games are played between two people:

It's your fault!
No, it's your fault!

It's my fault.
No, it's my fault.

It's your fault.
That's right. I'm bad, it's my fault. I'm sorry.
Well, you should be.

It's their fault.
That's right. If it weren't for them. . . .

It's my fault.
That's okay, honey. You can't help it. You're just not feeling well, (strong, lucky, smart) enough.

The healthier a couple gets, the quicker they move to an interaction like: I care.

Your care really helps, and let's do something about the problem.
Okay, let's.

Blame focuses on the past. The solution is in the future. The plan for the solution can be in the present, if we put it there. This awareness is very characteristic of highly functional couples. Blame, shame, guilt, and fault-finding all dodge the essential truth. If we want something to be better, we must decide on a plan of action, and we must act to carry it out. As a rancher-husband in my office once put it, "When the barn's on fire, let's spray water, not guilt." Healthy couples study the past to learn what they can do differently in the future.

In several translations Paul's description of love, in his first letter to the Corinthians, states, "Love rejoices in the truth" (I Corinthians 13:6). Highly love-functional couples do rejoice in the truth together. They have learned that truth helps them reach solutions that lead to successful living.

Unfortunately, codependent couples cooperate to deny happy, pleasant, positive truths. In a CoRecovery couples group a new couple was told, "I really like the way you two laugh and joke with each other." First, one of them replied, "Oh, but we fight a lot." And the other said, "We go for days without even talking to each other." Then they began to argue about that. Another group member pointed out they had been doing fine until they were praised. At that point they discovered how well they cooperated to deny happy, pleasant, positive truths. Soon, they saw their identity as a couple was in being a dysfunctional couple; and they were very fearfully dependent on that identity. It wasn't okay to be okay. There was a contradictory, irrational fear that if they got okay, they would split up. Even though accepting praise was hard for them for a long time, they worked on it and eventually became proficient in giving and receiving praise.

There are several other ways codependent couples cooperatively deny the truth they need. They suppress the truth by the false logic of rationalizing away evidence. They project a smoke screen of blame and shame. They also hide from the truth in addictions. Functioning as a healthy couple means jointly searching for the truth, continually working to improve understandings of the truth and, for the most part, enjoyably sharing the process. In this way couples grow more intimate, and that brings a sense of closeness. The denial in codependent couples leads to feelings of isolation and aloneness.

If you and your mate are reading this book with open and discriminating minds, you are taking excellent steps in exploring for truth. Beware of automatically accepting everything it says. Not everything will apply. Beware of automatically rejecting everything it says. Both those responses suggest denial at work. If you are reading this book together, talking about each part and working to synthesize your differing viewpoints can start you toward being a more love-functional couple.

Love Focused Self-Work and Systems Work

In our work with codependent couples, one sign of improvement consistently stands out as the beginning of solid growth. Both mates stop focusing on how their spouse should change. They begin to focus on how to improve themselves. Later they add how to improve the relationship itself. The accusatory use of the word "you" is reduced. It is replaced by the use of "I." Later, the softer spoken words "we" and "us" emerge. A blameful, "You started it!" becomes a thoughtful, "How did I help start it?" Later, an enthusiastic, "Let us really work at it." "We can do it now," may be added.

Sometimes, a person will try to fake it. With no intention of including themselves they say something like, "We should cut the lawn today," meaning, "You" should do this. As couples become more functional their voice tones change. Intonations of calm, loving thoughtfulness replace harsh and indifferent tones. A happy, "Let's try making love in the morning," replaces a complaining, "You always want to do it at night when I'm tired." This type of comment focuses on the systems solution instead of on individual blaming.

Even more common in codependency are attempts at taking care of our spouse's needs to the exclusion of our individual needs. This is another type of "you" focus which may be done by one or both mates. It is destructive although, at first, it can seem loving. Listen to this type of interaction:

Would you like to go someplace?
If you would, Dear.
Where would you like to go?
I don't care. Wherever you'd like to go.
Do you have any notions of what you'd like to do?
No, Dear, whatever you want is fine with me.
I can't really think of anything.
I'm sure you will and whatever it is will be just fine.

Healthy couples realize they do have preferences. Even if the preference is not a strong one they reveal it. "I think I'd like to eat Italian tonight." "That's okay, especially, if we can see a movie afterwards." "Do I get to pick the show or is it your turn?" This is a healthier conversation.

One problem with the first conversation is that it represents an abdication of responsibility masked as allowing the mate to have what he (or she) wants. Such compliant self-sacrifice makes everything take longer. No one is carrying the burden of decision making, or the burden is all on one person. Self-work is required in coupleship. Individuals must get in touch with their personal wants and contribute them to the relationship. Taking a stand, large or small, can feel risky or selfish. Codependent people often feel uncomfortable at first with self-dependent stands. As a couple grows healthier, assertions become fun. The assertion of a desire is a healthy self-love action. It exemplifies self-dependence instead of other-dependence. This self-dependence is a source of strength for couples.

Healthy couples are composed of people working on knowing their feelings, wants, and needs. They then add these to their mutual system of growth and development.

"I'd like to try my hand at sailing," she said. "Sounds good. Do you want company?" he said. "Sure," she said. Later, he said, "I'm really glad you brought sailing into our lives. I think it's one of the most enjoyable things we do together." She then added, "Ever since I learned to get in touch with my wants and to tell you about them, things have been going better between us. And I really appreciate your willingness to experiment with my wants."

Attempting to take care of another's needs and abandoning one's individual needs is not relating; it is caretaking. When people get strong they want to escape their caretakers. Healthfully relating couples build a system that supports independent growth without self-sacrifice, and that enriches the relationship.

Emotional Intercourse

Do you know what a feeling is? Do you know how it differs from a thought? Do you know thoughts and feelings are very different? Do you know that sharing natural feelings, or "emotional intercourse," is what a healthy mated relationship is mostly all about? Do you know that most feelings can be expressed with a single word while thoughts take whole sentences? Do you know that feelings are part of our internal guidance system, and each feeling has a different basic service it tries to accomplish for us? Do you know that to deny feelings and their guidance messages can lead to sickness or harm? Do you know that emotional feelings are just like physical feelings? Do you know that without sharing natural feelings a couple is not likely to make it?

Let us look at some simple examples. Feeling cold guides us to warm up, hungry to eat, tired to rest, hot to cool down, sleepy to sleep, and full to stop eating. Each has a specific guidance and each has but one word to label it. Natural emotional feelings work about the same. So-called bad feelings say change something, and natural good feelings say keep doing what you're doing. Fear guides us to seek safety. Comfort says stay where you are. Boredom indicates now is the time for something different. Anxiety suggests something not yet known is wrong; figure out what it is. Joy promotes fully doing what you are doing. Anger says get powerful. Some feelings are more complicated. Depression, for instance, guides us to be still and to take inventory of what's wrong. By the way, in depression what is most often wrong is love starvation.

A couple acting with good emotional intercourse communicates these guidance system messages. Then they know what is needed. Without the guidance of shared emotions a couple lacks an accurate road map to improvement.

Most couples afflicted with codependency know little about how to use the guidance systems of emotions, and that's tragic. They know even less about sharing emotions. It's important to understand, you have not shared your mate's feelings until you have felt something. Mere mental knowing is not sharing. You have to, sort of, feel it with them. Then you have to show your feeling, so they can perceive it.

Codependents are often out of touch with what they really feel, so they cannot share their real feelings. As they get in touch with their feelings they usually feel scared, and they fear sharing these feelings with their mates. Thus codependents often fight their real feelings. The road to healthy sharing is traveled with loving carefulness. Healthy couples do not fight feelings. They share them and get guidance from them. They also work to learn all they can about them. Hurt, by the way, says harm is on the way. Hurt is our friend, always trying to save us from harm. It is the hurt in many relationships that drives us to get help before it's too late.

Sharing the hurt is tremendously important to the continued existence of love relationships. In both love and health, hurt is our salvation. The most dangerous illnesses are the ones that never hurt; they just suddenly kill you. They are like the people who think everything is fine; then one day they come home to an empty house and a note saying, "I've left you." They never had hurt's guidance to help them improve. I like to tell couples, always help each other share the pain—it is the only fair and safe thing to do. Protecting you from my pain deprives you of the guidance message of my pain, and threatens our relationship.

Don't forget to share the good feelings too. Sharing the joy, being proud together, sharing sexy feelings, and all forms of feeling good enriches life together. The sharing of good feelings about yourself, your life, and your mate are very much a part of being a love-functional couple.

Because codependents often dam up their feelings, the dam sometimes bursts, and a flood of feelings can swamp a love relationship. Placid indifference turns suddenly to overwhelming depression or enormous anger. The flood can relieve the pressure of suppressed emotions. The buildup of suppressed emotions can lead to physical illness. This is because every emotion has biological components and effects. They are meant to be released in a controlled sort of way, much like engineers release reservoir waters through the floodgates of a dam. This keeps the dam from breaking, creates a reservoir of power, and yields irrigation where things grow. Likewise, healthy work with emotions does the same. Healthy couples help each other release emotional pressure. The reasonable, controlled release of these emotions generates information and motivation for improvement. As couples learn to do this, there is a reduction of depression, anxiety, anger, and loneliness. Mellowness, serenity, curiosity, delight, ecstacy, and a host of other up feelings come to take their place.

As a couple continues in CoRecovery work, they often find they have been dealing with their emotions through compulsive behaviors. Overeating, workaholism, overspending, obsessional sex or antisex thoughts or behaviors, hyperreligiosity and many other compulsive behaviors subvert the natural flow of emotions. Sometimes people switch from one compulsion to another. Good emotional intercourse is a great help in curing compulsions.

In emotional intercourse, a couple creates an atmosphere conducive to handling emotions. Emotions can rise to the surface of awareness where they can be fully experienced, identified, understood, shared, learned from, and released. As one man in CoRecovery put it:

> *My emotions used to make me nervous. I'd get real busy dodging the feelings, because I was afraid of them. Now, with my lover, I just let the feelings emerge in their own good time, and relax with that. I used to tell my lover, 'Don't cry, don't laugh so loud, don't be mad, don't be so boisterous, don't act so sexy, don't look so intense.' I guess I was telling her, 'Don't feel.' I was so afraid of her feelings, I tried to suppress them. In a way, I think my lover's feelings reminded me of all the emotions I was keeping down. Now I say, 'Come cry in my arms,' and I cry too. Today I laugh even louder than my lover. We really share the experience of our feelings now, and that's brought us so much closer. It's surprising how that eased all my nervousness. Now I don't have to do all my old compulsive stuff. That part's great, too.*

Good emotional intercourse means we take our most intimate parts, and expose them to each other. Then, as in good sex, these parts are lovingly felt, cherished, cared for. This leads to climaxes of emotional intimacy, closeness and feeling extremely loved. The healthier a couple grows, the more they know how to do this.

Sensing Safety: What Really Works

In many ways codependency is about trying to be safe in ways that just can't work. Codependent people don't love themselves enough to feel safe in relationships. This leads them to consistently believe that they are not lovable or loved. They too quickly believe they are in danger of losing their sources of love and potential love. From these beliefs flow a great many compulsive actions, a lot of anxiety, and a tendency toward hypervigilance. Many people in codependent relationships grew up in homes where love was only conditionally given and often very suddenly and erratically withdrawn. As children, they felt anxiety about love and developed compulsions to stay safe, to stifle their love pain. A watchful sensitivity to mood shifts grew along with this. All this was done to survive the ravages of love starvation.

Until fairly recently, we did not understand that love deprivation has a very detrimental effect on our neurochemistry. It can even cause death in otherwise well-cared-for infants (Montagu 1975). We know love delivered too infrequently can interfere with the growth process and even cause dwarfism (Talbot 1947). More recently, research with adults has revealed that disturbances in how love is experienced can trigger many imbalances in body chemistry, resulting in serious illness and even death (Siegel 1989). Is it any wonder codependency is filled with anxiety, hypervigilance, and compulsive behaviors which attempt to counterbalance love deficiencies? Chemical addiction itself may be just such an attempt.

In healthy, love-functional couples, a sense of safety grows in an entirely different way. Self-love is fostered by the couple's love. The couple supports each other's growth of self-caring actions and attitudes. Self-sacrifice is discouraged. The couple understands that love means actively desiring the well-being of their loved ones. Self-sacrifice is only for times in which they cannot figure out an "I win, you win" solution. In codependency, there is frequent and usually needless self-sacrifice to achieve a sense of safety. Compare these two interactions:

Codependent Couple:

She: *I've about decided not to go to college this semester, though I really want to. But I think you and the kids need me more, so I guess I'll stay home again.*
He: *That's right, Dear. You are a mother and a wife first.*

What is a Love-Healthy Couple?

Love-Functional Couple:

She: *I've about decided to go to college this semester because it will do me a lot of good. I think it will help me be a better person, and that will help me be a better everything else.*
He: *Go for it. The kids and I can take up the slack. We'll have lively discussions about what you are learning and we can all stand the fresh input.*

In the love-functional couple, what helps an individual grow, develop, and become more is welcomed as an addition to the couple. In codependency, one mate adding to himself (or herself) is all-too-often seen as a subtraction from the other. From healthy self-development grows healthy self-love. From this grows a sense of, "I am worthy, intrinsically of value and, therefore, I'm lovable." This shows an inner- or self-dependent sense of safety. If I can see that I am lovable, I can conclude that even if I lost you (which I'd hate) I'd still be lovable. Therefore, I would not have to let myself remain love starved forever. My safety is in knowing I can get the love I need. I'm not outer- or other-dependent for this. My loveability will attract other sources of love, and my healthy self-love can get me through periods of not being loved by others. I'm safe. One CoRecovery mate summed this up by saying, "When I got over needing you, I was finally free to choose you because I wanted you. When I needed you, it wasn't a choice; it was a sick need."

A Team for Health

Codependent couples often live in a teamwork that promotes illness. Increasingly, love-functional couples work as a team to live healthfully.

Typically in codependent relationships, one or both partners act to support the other in one or more forms of substance abuse. Alcohol, mood-altering chemicals (including prescription drugs), smoking, and food consumption are commonly overdone. Oh, there may be occasional, or even frequent, talk of cutting back on this or that, but little is accomplished. The sedation and booster effects of various substances are used instead of improving the love relationship itself. Dependence on such substances means the couple stagnates and deteriorates. With substance abuse, illness and accident susceptibility grows. In love-functional couples, a proactive teamwork against substance abuse is increasingly typical. Among codependent couples inactivity or antihealth activity is much more common, accompanied by a lot of denial.

It is very stressful to live in a codependent relationship. Consequently, stress-related illnesses are common. Both partners may eventually break down physically. Denial keeps the couple behaving in the same old way, often until it is too late.

By becoming a team for health, love-functional couples tend to balance love, work and play. Joining together to promote adequate relaxation, fun, exercise, diet, sexuality, and love (that great stress fighter), helps couples live healthier.

Physical abuse, behavioral abuse, and psychological abuse are all too common in couples severely afflicted by codependency. The couple's codependent interactions after abusive episodes are usually full of denial. Thus, the violent actions, the sexual, monetary, and property violations, the severe attacks on self-esteem, the emotional manipulations and "mind games" are all minimized, excused or dealt with through blame instead of change. This reinforces the likelihood of more abuse and too often the result is broken bodies, broken minds, and broken hearts.

Seeing couples leave all these abusive actions behind is great. Watching them promote each other's physical and psychological health is a joy. I teach most couples with severe physical abuse problems to start with the decision that they will touch each other only with love, never anger, never abuse or misuse. They learn that real love is constructive, not destructive; therefore, acts that can destroy or harm do not come from love. Starting with this, even severely afflicted couples begin to grow their teamwork for health.

Proactive teamwork for health is an acquired set of behaviors. According to our cultural training, health is what you have by way of luck; or healthy is what your physician makes you after you are sick. Now, we are learning health has to be maintained by our actions. Health is not just a lack of illness. It is a state of being vitally alive and functioning optimally. Health takes work, but it's worth it. Love-functional couples do the work of health because they want to be vitally alive and functioning optimally in each other's lives.

Newness and Renewal

There is a terrible tendency for couples lost in their codependency to keep doing the same old things. They avoid anything new, fresh or different. Healthy couples seek new experiences, fresh input, different people and situations. One of the things we frequently say to couples starting their CoRecovery process is:

Do the same old thing, and you will get the same old results. Do something new and you will get new results. The new results may be worse or they may be better. But at least you have a chance for something better.

Without new ideas, new situations, new attempts, new methods, new changes, renewal is impossible. Codependent couples keep doing the same old things because they seem safe, but they are not. Stagnation leads to deterioration, which leads to destruction, which leads to death. Healthy, love-functional couples are into growth that results in fresh, shared actions, thoughts and feelings.

Love-functional couples are much quicker to seek help from books, consultants, friends, schools, counselors and other sources. Codependents fear new input will harm them, so they stick with worn-out, stale ways that offer less and less. This week, codependent couples are doing about what they did last week, last month, last year and last decade, if they last that long. A major discovery was made in a massive comparison of healthy and unhealthy families. Healthy families kept changing, doing things differently, and giving themselves the enrichment of variety. Unhealthy families changed little, until they self-destructed (Beavers 1977).

As couples continue their CoRecovery, they get comfortable with change, with exploring the new, and with experimenting with the different. They become uncomfortable with stagnating sameness.

Sex for Love and Love for Sex

Codependency does not support a healthful sex life. Generally speaking, there is one problem or another. Healthy couples also can have sex problems. However, if they do a good job of loving each other as they love themselves, they get past their sex problems faster than codependents do. Codependent couples can overcome their sex problems too. For some of these couples, doing this is one of the hardest jobs they tackle. Commonly, couples dealing with codependency issues are out of balance about sex. Some behave hypersexually, some nonsexually, some antisexually and some alternate among these behaviors. Compulsiveness is frequently in evidence along with these behaviors, until love takes over.

One client said in a CoRecovery group, "When I finally began to feel I loved myself and my mate loved me too, my insistence on having sex morning, noon and night started diminishing." Similarly, another client added, "I really was antisexual, though I hid that from myself. I just had to be a part of every antipornography, antirape, antihomosexual, antilesbian, antinudity, antianything sexual group there was. Now, I realize I was afraid of sex, so I attacked it. I was especially afraid of my sexuality. My poor codependent husband got so he was afraid to move at night. He was sure I'd accuse him of wanting to rape me. I was even getting where I saw all touch as sexual and perverted. Now I see that was a perversion itself. I started getting better when I heard how much the women in this group liked, or were learning to like, sex. I saw that liking sex was a part of liking and loving themselves. I had to admit it wasn't everybody else, it was me. I had to learn to love my sexual self and my man's sexual self. Was I ever scared. But I did it, and am I glad. I'm also real glad for my husband's loving help, and this group's loving help."

Sex, like a candlelight dinner, can be a way to show and experience love. Sex can also be like junk food at the local fast-food place, more deleterious than nutritious. To do well sexually, we have to treat both ourselves and our mates with love. It's beneficial to soak in the love we are given along with the sexuality. Feeling well-loved is often what it takes for couples to let go of their bad programming about sex, loose their inhibitions, and really enjoy sexuality.

Love is a great addition to sexuality. Without healthy self-love and without healthy love of others, sexuality sometimes seems to go in harmful directions. One CoRecovering woman said to her mate:

"It's your love and it's my new self-love that brought me back from my slavery to violent sex. Now gentleness and silliness can turn me on. Before, it took seeing some man in pain. I'm a woman now, not a 'sicko' and it's love that did it."

Healthy couples work to mix their love with sex and their sex with love.

Healthy Spirituality

One of the best things about Twelve Step programs is the emphasis on spiritual awakening. Terms like "higher power" and "God as we understand him" have been a great help in assisting people to not get bogged down in dogma and religious controversy. Couples who work together to have a healthy spiritual life do much better, but there are traps to avoid. Some of these traps can be expressed as (1) being religious without being spiritual; (2) making dogma your god; (3) being codependent on a church, cleric or some other element of religion; and (4) being stuck in immature or sick religion.

Codependent couples looking for safety sometimes become enmeshed in religion rather than having a spiritual awakening. "Spiritual" and "religious" are not the same thing. I am a health specialist and speak only as one. Spirituality, when it's well done, helps couples become healthier.

Poorly done, it can be very destructive. In our CoRecovery program we have created some guidelines for developing healthy spirituality. These guidelines were developed with the assistance of some of our interns who had seminary backgrounds and the religious and theological references they used (Lyon 1957; Ferm 1985; Kant 1934).

1. Healthful spirituality is full of love, based on love, and is love active. Guilt, shame, imposition of belief systems, control, fear, dependency and a host of other negatives characterize some peoples' experiences with religion. These are not love based and do not constitute healthy spirituality. Couples who are a team working together at spiritual growth, do so lovingly, not dogmatically, insistently, nor fearfully. Healthy spirituality aids a couple's approach to sharing and growing love.

2. Healthful spirituality involves a democratic, ongoing, searching exploration into that which is greater than ourselves. Healthy couples can believe very differently from one another. They can be a loving team assisting one another make their own spiritual discoveries, and have their own spiritual experiences. Codependent insecurity in couples can result in artificial sameness. Healthy means there is room for individual differences, change, new development, and growth.

3. Healthy spirituality involves a sensitivity to that which is mystic. This includes awe, mystery, wonder, astonishment, exaltation, solemnity, universality, inspiration, and reverence. Sharing these, couples experience amazing closeness and a great sense of intimate, powerful love. The anxiety present in codependency and the desire for the safety of the mundane often preclude couples from searching, finding, or sharing mystical experiences.

4. Healthy spirituality includes a commitment to truth wherever it is found. Denial is characteristic of codependency and addiction. Scientific and historical evidence and understandings do not threaten healthy spirituality. In fact, they aid and enhance spiritual searching. Healthy couples can present each other with various versions of their respective truths, and lovingly deal with them without fear. Codependent couples feel tense and threatened by concepts, understandings, and evidence which differs from their own. Healthy couples can be okay with ideas like, "We see through a glass differently," and, "We see different things through different glasses."

5. Healthy spirituality is in accord with the principles of health, human nature, and psychological wellness. Couples who are increasing their spiritual growth tend to see nature and the part of nature which is health as manifestations of the spiritual. Codependency turns couples toward antinatural, antipsychological and antihealthful teachings because they offer a false sense of security. This can lead to ruin. Many a cult and many a sick religious group has preyed upon codependents. That's because codependents submit to authority figures and authoritative dictates in order to feel safe. Such dictates fly in the face of natural laws, especially those pertaining to health. Healthy natural sexuality, curiosity, diet, fun, experimentation, and the like can be part of a healthy couple's spirituality. Religious training that constantly helps people feel at war with their nature, and nature in general, works against the development of healthy spirituality.

6. Healthful spirituality aids ethical development. The way a spiritually developing couple treats each other and others is increasingly honest, devoid of deceit, manipulation, hiding, cheating, or other unethical practices. Because of their insecurity codependent couples lie to each other directly and by omission. If temporary control or safety can be achieved by deceit, it is; and it is rationalized away. "It was for their own good," is a common rationalization by the codependent. Couples becoming healthfully love functional increasingly give up a dependency on deceit and other less ethical behaviors. They often report their awakening spirituality helped them do this.

7. Healthful spirituality excludes reliance on magic and superstition. Couples often improve their teamwork for spirituality when they study what magic and superstition really are. One starter concept is that magic and superstition involve attempts at manipulating rather than relating to a higher power and the spiritual universe. Both, of course, help the insecure feel falsely safe, and codependents manipulate outcomes for a sense of safety.

8. Healthful spirituality does not rely on literal mythology, sacred places, symbols, or objects. These things may aid healthful spirituality as representations of greater truths. Couples improve their spirituality by reading together the spiritual understandings of others. They may discover the great truths embodied in certain stories and history by talking together. Certain objects, places and symbols may have special spiritual significance to them. Picayune insistence on only their interpretation or understanding, however, is something healthy mates do

not attempt to inflict on each other. This only divides them, no matter how well-meaning the motivation is.

9. Healthful spirituality is inclusive, not exclusive. Spirituality frequently helps couples feel that they are a part of each other, that they are related to everyone and all of life. Systems that help individuals or couples feel superior to others, or in other words, "We're okay, they're not" block or trivialize spiritual experience. Small, mean spirited, condescending, demeaning, egocentric attitudes result from the "We're okay, they're not" school of thought. These attitudes of exclusivity definitely retard a couple's spiritual health.

Love Learning, Love Growing

Love-functional couples keep functional by continuing to expand their knowledge and practice of love. Like good farmers, they keep acquiring new and better ways of growing their crops. Unfortunately, codependent couples keep relying on what their families taught them about love. They also rely on our society's old destructive misconceptions about love. Actually, many of the ancient Greek, Eastern, and Biblical understandings of love fit well with modern discoveries. Sadly, our societal concepts came mostly from the Dark Ages, when the knowledge of the ancients was lost to the majority.

Right now, you are learning about love. Later in Chapters Five, Six and Seven which cover the eight ways of demonstrating love, you are going to learn how to grow love as a couple. To mentally learn, however, is not enough. You must practice what you learn. Healthy couples practice what they know to do about love, and stay healthy by doing so. Codependent couples start coming out of their codependency when they begin looking for new ways to grow love. It is a mistake to believe if love goes wrong, just find someone new, and they will give you all the love you need. Hunting for love does not work nearly as well as growing it. Growing love takes learning new ways, and then practicing those new ways. That's next. Let's proceed.

Part Two

CoRecovery

CoRecovery . . . 4

Can We Jump Start Our Love?

Now we'll look at the first steps to reducing codependency and becoming a fully love-functional couple. Couples start toward CoRecovery when at least one of them decides they need or could use improvement. This desire for improvement is the first step. It can be a mild, medium, or an extremely strong desire. Pain in any degree, a vague or strong suspicion that something is wrong, boredom with sameness, or the natural want for improvement can spark this desire. At least some degree of hope comes next. Almost all couples who have at least a little hope can make substantial gains if they learn to use the ways that work.

After desire and hope come study and communication. Studying what has already worked for other couples can shorten the process of improvement. Custom-tailoring successful methods to fit your situation begins right after that, and continues throughout your life together. Finding new ways to show and receive love and creating improvements are part of what being a love-functional couple is all about.

You may however be asking, "Who is CoRecovery for? Does it apply to us?" Let's look at that.

Is CoRecovery For You?

A few years ago, a very worried John and Julie came into my office. John said, " Maybe you won't want to work with us, we are not married." Julie added, "We're not living together either." John then said, "We don't know if we really love each other, or not. We may just be addicted to one another, or to sex; maybe we're infatuated. We can't figure out what we are." Julie said, "We've heard about your couple's program, but there are some reasons you might not want to work with us as a couple." "And those are?" I asked. John somewhat defensively said, "I've been sleeping with another woman," as he fearfully glanced at Julie. She lowered her head and sheepishly said, "You might as well know it all. Me too—I mean, well. . . I've been seeing another woman too." In a shy whisper Julie added, "I'm bisexual, but more and more I just want to be with John. But I'm not sure." Then John said, "You won't take us in your couples program, right?" I asked, "Do you both regard yourselves as a couple?" Both simultaneously and strongly said, "Yes!" "Then let's give it a try," I said. Now a child is on the way, and they say they could not be doing better. It took a lot of work, but today in some ways they live rather like a traditional couple and in some ways not. One way they are different is they are happier than average.

Couples define themselves, as I see it, through a rather natural process. In CoRecovery, and in other couples counseling programs at our center, we take everybody who identifies themselves as a couple. Married, unmarried, living together or not, heterosexual, homosexual, bisexual, transsexual, or unable to have sex, mixed races and religions, disabled, retarded or any other combination does not exclude them from being a couple. They all have the same kinds of couples problems, patterns, systems, ways of failing and succeeding, and all the rest of the psychosocial dynamics of being a couple. They may have some special additional difficulties, but the basics are the same. So if you and your mate see your relationship as that of a couple, and you think you have codependency issues, CoRecovery is for you. If you join a CoRecovery couples group, you will probably meet couples just like you in more ways than not.

Our inclusive approach to couples corresponds to the statistics of our modern world. Barbara Vobejda of the Washington Post reports that one third of all women in the U.S., under 45, reply that they have cohabited without being married. Between the ages of 25 and 30, the number rises to 45 percent according to her report citing The National Center for Health Statistics (1991). More and more couples are custom-tailoring their love lives; some choose not to use a state government's contract for how to be a couple. Others do not totally accept a religious institution's regulations but instead customize their relationship's rules. Nevertheless they operate within the natural laws of love.

Real mate love, false forms of love, and codependency problems can exist in the relationship of almost any two people. In working with literally thousands of couples of all types, and backgrounds, I find the presence of real mate love is what makes the difference. Therefore all couples are welcome in CoRecovery.

GAINING THE ESSENTIAL START-UP KNOWLEDGE TOGETHER

By reading this book at least one of you has already started toward CoRecovery. You have begun to acquire the necessary start-up knowledge.

Can We Jump Start Our Love?

Of course, to really make it CoRecovery, you and your mate will have to interact. Like every team both of you will do best by sharing the same knowledge base. When partners in a mated relationship do not share enough of the same knowledge, teamwork suffers. This is true of all teams. Really good football teams spend a lot of time studying their play books, orchestras learn the score, and surgical teams study the procedures. Virtually every high-performance team spends a lot of time acquiring, sharing and communicating mutual knowledge. Until recently these teamwork concepts have not been applied to couples. One reason is we just did not have enough really useful knowledge about successful couples. Now we have much information, and more and more couples are making use of it. So the next step you take can be sharing the knowledge in this book, and really communicating thoroughly about it.

To do that a few words of caution are in order. Codependency patterns in couples sometimes cause blame fights, manipulations of guilt, and various put-downs using new knowledge. Remember, anything that can be used can be misused. "I win, you win, the problem loses" is the only solution worth having. Sharing the knowledge does not mean using it to control, to justify, or to help your mate feel bad.

I have seen couples get started using the knowledge in this book in a rich variety of ways. Here are some of them:

1. Read aloud to each other, never at each other.

2. Both of you highlight or underline in different colors. Hand the book back and forth, noting what the other has seen as important. Do not use this to tell them what they should do. That is behaving 'at' not 'with' your mate.

3. Write in the margins and blank spaces, conveying your understanding of what is meant, then read each other's notes. Don't fight over them.

4. Using pieces of paper, add pages to the book to suggest how you both can apply different ideas from the book to your relationship.

5. Use two copies of the book to each read, underline, and write notes. Then trade the two copies and reread it, noting what is written and underlined.

6. While reading talk into a tape recorder stating what is most important to you, and record the questions you most want answered. After you

have finished the book, review the questions to see if you have found answers.

7. Set time aside to talk about what you are reading, and lovingly share and plan your growth.

These are ways to jointly work with this knowledge and with each other. Working in these ways helps couples grow their closeness and improve their team spirit.

If your mate is reluctant to read this book, or to do some of the work suggested for whatever reason, I have a suggestion. Read this section aloud to your mate and ask your mate to experiment for a week or two with just a few of these teamwork behaviors. Run this experiment with a good attitude for the sake of the team.

It Takes Practice, Practice, Practice

Remember when you learned to drive a car? If you are like me, you killed the engine, got confused, got scared and certainly did not do well at first. Like bike riding, swimming and a host of other things, if you practiced enough it all got "natural." Now you just do it. Well, the same thing goes for learning to rid your relationship of codependency habits and fill it with love habits.

At first you will not get it right, then you will some of the time, and then more of the time. You will never be perfect and that is great! It is great because it means you can keep growing. It is important you both lovingly let each other be awkward, forget, make mistakes and generally mess up your new efforts at learning to love more effectively. Remember, never play the psychological, dysfunctional game, "Strike one, you're out, the game's over." Like everything humans do which is important and ongoing, it takes joining together in practice, practice, practice.

Couples Learning From Couples

Couples together can do a lot to help themselves improve, in addition to reading and practicing on their own. We humans can learn so much from one another. People who grow up in families learn from each other. Unfortunately, some families are teaching the wrong lessons. Other families just do not know how to teach the right lessons about love and living together. To make up for these family deficits several kinds of groups have been developed.

Let's take a look at group learning. Some people fear groups. Fears of being exposed, losing control to others, and embarrassment have to be put aside to gain the great enrichment that comes from group learning, practice, feedback, comradery, and modeling. Unless we learn from each other, we are stuck in the proverbial having-to-reinvent-the-wheel situation. Down the street somebody has already invented it; and in a group they will show you how to use it. Do not rely on just learning by yourself. Joint learning is partly what makes a couple so great. Learning from other couples is an extension of that process. Here are some guidelines to enhance your learning and growing experiences in groups.

Build friendship networks. Build or grow an informal, but deep and real, friendship network. It is deep if you can cry together. It is real if you tell each other things you will not tell acquaintances. One of the most common things codependent couples do is isolate themselves from deep and real contact with others. This effectively shuts off one of the best sources of real knowledge in deep, personal, intimate areas, where you need it most. Good friends share books and the ideas they read in them. Tapes and videos about couples' relationships can also be shared this way.

Form a study group. Form a study group to read and talk about this book. Such a group can be a step to forming a friendship network. Many couples already have met together to study this material and have made considerable gains.

Join or form a couples support group. Support groups that work well go deeper and are much more supportive than study groups. A few words of caution are important here. If you can, it is far better to be in a group together as a couple rather than separately. The two of you simultaneously gaining the same knowledge and sharing the same experiences help the most. If you can't do this together, one of you joining is better than neither.

Attend seminars and retreats. Go together to seminars, workshops, and, best of all, retreats, where couples are dealt with as couples. Weekend retreats that focus on the new knowledge about love have been responsible for incredible breakthroughs and wonderful advancements in the lives of couples. Going separately can help, but going together is more likely to lead to togetherness. At such retreats, time apart is often provided, as well as time together. Sometimes couples find a full-fledged weekend, or week-long retreat a bit overwhelming to start with. That is okay. There are a growing number of one-hour lectures, and one-evening workshops given by schools, hospitals, churches, clinics and special organizations. Watch your newspaper for announcements. Call any psychiatric hospital or treatment center and you will probably be able to get on a mailing list.

Join a Twelve Step group. This is a fine way to start learning about codependence and related issues. CoDa (Co-Dependents Anonymous - see Appendix) will open all sorts of doors. It operates in the Alcoholics Anonymous tradition and many of the members belong to other Twelve Step groups. CoDa exists to help men and women with their codependency problems in relationships. There are over 2000 CoDa groups in thirteen countries, which is pretty amazing considering CoDa was not started until 1986. CoDa groups are well-structured support groups. Like all organizations, some of their groups are better than others. To evaluate one, determine if there seems to be both a spirit of and a focus on love. Also check to see if there is an emphasis on staying together rather than splitting up.

All couples must help themselves. Joining with others who are doing the same can be a great boon to your self-help efforts. Now, let us look at more powerful ways to improve.

What About Professional Help?

Self-help alone may not help enough. If your relationship seems really stuck in a dysfunctional codependency system, get professional help. If your relationship seems to be deteriorating rapidly, get professional help. If your mate or your relationship seems to be in some sort of danger, get professional help. And if you just happen to desire the fastest and most effective way of growing your relationship, get professional help.

Now, all professional help is not equal. In fact, the wrong professional help can be a great waste, and sometimes even counterproductive. The first thing to know is that a great many counselors and therapists, including psychologists, psychiatrists, psychotherapists and psychoanalysts, are well trained to help individuals but not couples, as such. If they want to treat you more separately than together, your relationship may be more harmed than helped. I once led a group conducting a series of studies comparing different forms of marital treatment (Cookerly 1976). I followed that work with a long-range follow-up. The results were very clear. The more couples were treated separately, the more they tended to separate and divorce (Cookerly 1980). Research by other professionals resulted in similar findings (Gurman 1981). Joint treatment, where your relationship itself can be dealt with directly, is something you can insist on. To find professionals who know how to do this, you may wish to consult your Yellow Pages.

Under Marriage Counseling you can usually find a listing for Clinical Members of the American Association for Marriage and Family Therapy. Now some of these therapists are far more trained in family therapy than they are in couples therapy, and there can be a big difference. So you have to ask them if they specialize in couples and not just families. You can find other professionals who have expertise in working with couples; be sure to ask. Credentials vary widely, so refer to *A Directory of Credentials in Counseling and Psychotherapy* (Martin and Cookerly 1989). And you can refer to the Resources Appendix of this book.

There is a small but rapidly growing number of chemical dependency and addictions counselors learning how to do CoRecovery work with couples. They often have a more complete understanding of codependency. But unless they have been trained in couples work itself, and CoRecovery approaches specifically, they may not know how to counsel you and your mate for better teamwork. There are licensed professional counselors, social workers, psychiatric nurses, pastoral counselors, and other counseling and therapy professionals who are learning how to do couples CoRecovery work.

You may find or have already found a counselor you feel good with. However, they may not know yet of CoRecovery approaches. They may be unaware of the new knowledge about love upon which CoRecovery is partly founded. If this is true, just ask your counselor or therapist to contact us and we will be glad to send them information (see the Resources Appendix of this book).

Another way to get help is to call your local addictions treatment center or psychiatric hospital. While it is true most psychiatrists are not trained in couples work, some of the other counselors working there may be. They may also offer special treatment programs in codependency. Even so, ask if they have special programs for couples, not just individuals or families. If they do not, suggest they call us. My staff and I have had a lot of experience helping other counselors, therapists, counseling centers, clinics, hospitals and treatment centers begin CoRecovery programs.

Well-developed professional help can include the option of being a member of a CoRecovery Couples therapy group. Not all couples choose this option, nor is it appropriate for all couples. However, for many, a Couples CoRecovery group offers the most powerful, most effective, most thorough and most complete way to effect healthful growth. It takes well-trained professional leadership and consistent, hard, challenging work, and it gets results. So, if you are inquiring about professional help, ask if there is a CoRecovery couples group available.

The research results on the effectiveness of couples groups is quite good. Codependency, as an independent concept, is not very old. Most of the published studies go back to its original inclusion with addictions problems. A host of these studies show that couples joint counseling, and couples group counseling, got better results than counseling without those forms of treatment (O'Farrell, Cutter & Floyd 1985; McCrady 1986; Zweben, Pearlman & Selina 1988).

FOCUSING ON LOVE

The most important part of getting started has to do with focusing on learning and practicing the ways of love. A lot of people have studied what is wrong, but only recently have people started to understand what is right in human relationships. The importance of knowing what's right is especially true when we consider the subject of love. Finally we can provide couples with a positive knowledge of love and that is making an enormous difference. All too many couples have discovered that books, educators and therapists know how to help them see what is wrong, what does not work, and what feels bad, but not the opposite.

Love and love knowledge works, if you and your mate work at using it. Love work is not so much a pulling of the "weeds" (problems) as it is a growing of the "flowers" (solutions and enrichments). Dr. George Pransky, an eminent marital therapist, in his book *Divorce Is Not The Answer* tells couples not to deal with the problems, and not to be caught up in what he calls "low mood therapy" He finds that "high mood therapy" and learning to transcend problems, works much more positively (1990). Love work is very "high mood," and is full of empowerment and the transcendence of problems.

To help you get started and to go further with CoRecovery, I suggest you keep focusing on love. One way couples can do this is to start a personal love journal. Write down everything you come to understand about love. Record experiences you have together that help you feel loving and loved, or anything else that seems pertinent. Some couples include drawings, diagrams, poems, artwork, meaningful greeting cards, love notes, photos, letters and other mementos of their joint adventures into love. A personal love journal can be a combination of a diary, study notes and a scrapbook. I suggest jointly making daily entries for two months. You can also write love notes to each other and even to yourself. After a week review together what you have written. Such reviews often lead to very new and different understandings. You might see common threads that you may not have noticed before. After the first two months you may want to switch to weekly or monthly entries, and then to write just when the fancy strikes you.

Can We Jump Start Our Love?

Creating your love library is another way to focus on love. Factual useful books about love are starting to appear. If this is your first book that focuses on love, your library of love just got started. One couple I know has started a video library of films that show healthy love relationships. In my house you can see a great many statuettes showing couples, families and others behaving lovingly. There are funny ones, ugly ones, beautiful ones, schmaltzy ones, just about everything, except expensive ones. They help me and my Beloved study love in an artistic, right brain sort of way.

However you and your mate choose to do it, be sure you find ways to focus on love learning. I remember a couple in our CoRecovery program. Regarding love learning, Sam said, "Theresa and I went to a hell of a lot of therapists, and got in a hell of a lot of treatment programs. The more we learned, the more hell we gave each other. Everybody told us to give it up. Then we landed in this CoRecovery couples stuff. That's when we finally learned something about love. We ain't giving each other hell no more, that's for sure." Theresa added, "I know it's corny, but because of this love-learning stuff, we have actually had a few moments of heaven. I think we might even know enough to have some more."

One last concept is important for getting off to a good, fresh start at CoRecovery. Only you and your mate can decide which of these ways is appropriate to your situation and your present way of being a couple. Get started in whatever ways you find best. If what you're doing isn't enough, add another way. Keep that up until the problems are resolved. If you are codependent, I know you can do this. Codependents have learned how to survive and keep going for long periods. Now the job is to turn that survivor strength into love-achievement strength. How do I know that? It is what I had to do and it is what most codependent couples I work with have to do.

CoRecovery . . . 5

How Do We Grow Intimate Love?

An individual, couple, or family that discovers how to end codependent behaviors has not magically discovered how to start giving and receiving love. For healthy love to flourish, the acts that show love must be learned, practiced, and consistently improved. The void created by no longer being or acting codependent must be filled by healthy, positive love actions that demonstrate the internal state of loving another. The way this is best explained is through a metaphor:

> *It is not enough to pull weeds in the human garden. If all we do is pull the weeds, we end up with a garden full of holes in which new weeds will grow. What we really must do is plant flowers, trees, and crops of love and bring them to fruition. Such a crop will push out and keep out the weeds, allowing the human garden to nourish and fill us.*

Some approaches to defeating the problems of codependency stress this weed-pulling aspect. But this isn't a solution that allows couples to flourish. What is needed instead is a crop of love, developed by learning and practicing just how people show love and become a love action team.

THE VITAL DIFFERENCES - CODEPENDENCY OR REAL LOVE?

"Good Loving" is vastly different from the behaviors that flow from dysfunctional codependency. The romance, the sexuality, the emotional intimacy, and the healthful bonding of good loving are also quite different. Couples who learn and practice the real behaviors of healthy love in teamwork with each other demonstrate powerful and joyous improvements over their old codependent behaviors.

Many people naively think that codependents are quite good at giving love. People think their only difficulty is that they have problems because they choose bad mates as a result of programming in their childhood. It is true they do, all too often, choose mates who are themselves dependent on some form of addiction or who are immature, often narcissistic, poor and inconsistent at love, and prone to substance abuse of one kind or another. These beliefs lead to the easy-sounding solution often suggested to people suffering the agonies of codependency: "Divorce your current spouse and learn to make better choices." Many have followed this advice—only to discover that nothing really got better as a result.

Would that things were so simple! The deeper problem facing many codependent people is learning just how healthy love really works. While in their hearts they may be quite loving, they usually know little about how to participate in truly mature love. People programmed to be codependent need a lot of work on how to grow past their misconceptions and unworkable, backfiring patterns of love interaction. They are more like their mates than is obvious at first glance. Both are quite codependent although in somewhat different ways. The good news is that both can learn just how healthy love is enacted.

How do we know what constitutes healthy love behavior? Well, first we are indebted to the massive research effort of Dr. Clifford Swenson, a social psychologist, and his scientific team (1972).* Swenson's research found that this thing we call love was very real and very necessary for life itself. For example, there is the work of Dr. Henry Chapin, a pediatrician who discovered that every single infant under two years of age placed in ten well-known orphanages in the U.S. before 1915 died. Moreover, they kept dying until further research revealed that they needed more than food and medicine to survive. They needed loving attention (Chapin 1915).

A comparative animal psychologist named Dr. Harry Harlow reproduced these results in a laboratory, studying infant monkeys. Those who were denied the love behaviors of other primates, failed to thrive, became sick, and did not respond well to treatment until love actions were reintroduced into their lives. Moreover, if they were given just enough love to stay alive, they had stunted physical development, were sexually maladapted, and could not form mated relationships with other monkeys (1971).

* The first major stage of his research obtained data from over 1,500 people, ages seventeen to eighty. Later replications of his work added several thousand more people to the number of subjects studied. The subjects demonstrated that at least 383 distinctive behaviors of showing love to a person could be identified. These 383 were treated by a complicated form of statistical analysis and subsequently seven major categories of demonstrating love were discovered. Clinical adaptations were made of Swenson's seven categories. Later, in clinical studies when these seven were used in attempts to teach people the behaviors of love, an eighth was discovered by my research and then added to training and therapy programs.

This was the beginning of work showing that without adequate love, severe, even life-threatening, dysfunction occurs. For example, a study at Massachusetts General Hospital, under the direction of Dr. N. B. Talbot, showed that the only similar abnormality in a group of 51 dwarfs was a certain pattern of inconsistent loving in their early life (1947). Soon after, other physiological research linked anorexia, various emotional disturbances, and several other forms of dysfunction to chemical imbalances in the brain that could only be attributed to inconsistent love patterns in early life.

Later research has linked a vast number of human physical problems to being poorly loved, not only in childhood but also in adulthood. Susceptibility to chemical and behavioral addictions, our ability to fight off disease, and many of our mental health problems are now thought to be related to chemical imbalances in our brains and bodies, that are in turn related to whether we give and receive the behaviors of love.

A healthy, long sex life, a life lived to the full, a life of great happiness and productivity is also linked to a continuous feedback loop of ongoing love behaviors. Clearly, the way we are loved changes our brain chemistry, and that changes the way we live and function every day of our lives. And now recovery, healing from even the most deadly of diseases, is being linked to the way people enact the major behaviors of love. Dr. Bernie Siegel, a noted oncology surgeon who has devoted his life to helping patients fight cancer, says, "If I told patients to raise their blood levels of immune globulins or killer T-cells, [items in our body that fight cancer] no one would know how. But if I can teach them to love themselves and others fully, the same changes happen automatically. The truth is: love heals" (1986, 181).

In our Couples CoRecovery Program, we are discovering the same thing—learning to love heals the ravages of codependency. The question, of course, is: how do we learn to love?

EIGHT WAYS WE SHOW LOVE

Dr. Swenson, lead scientist of the massive and often-replicated investigation into how humans show each other love, discovered that communicating love involved a limited number of differing but intertwined groups of behavior.

Couples in our CoRecovery program who learn and practice these forms of loving behavior report amazing changes in their lives as couples. They also demonstrate how these ways of showing love reduce and even eliminate their codependent behaviors, helping them avoid divorce or permanent separation from their mates.

Unfortunately, because many counselors who first started treating codependency had not found ways to help a couple as a couple, many codependents became single in their effort to escape their destructive love relationship patterns. Treatment as a couple, where both are learning the same things together in the same place at the same time is usually crucial, if the couple is to have a chance to survive as a couple. Learning apart from each other, at best, results in the couple not knowing how to coordinate their interactions. Individual treatment may lead to individual growth, but more commonly the couple grows apart. This is because the teamwork training to show and receive the behaviors of love together is missing. Many sad, often tragic, unnecessary breakups are the result of this inability to establish a feedback loop of coordinated love efforts. Even if they love each other, a couple's efforts at love may be futile unless they learn to coordinate loving behaviors through teamwork. Learning love teamwork is just as important as learning teamwork in any team sport or performance art.

To help understand the eight major ways we show love, consider the first three ways as *loving internal states* (here in Chapter 5) and the next four ways as *outward physical manifestations of loving* (Chapter 6). The eighth way of loving (Chapter 7) is a catalyst that makes the other seven ways succeed in relationships and is therefore discussed separately.

Let us now start learning at least the basics of the major ways humans can learn to love each other. Let us also take a look at how these varied ways of demonstrating love differ from codependency behaviors. And each time we examine one of the forms of love, we will look at the health benefits they produce in our bodies, particularly the benefits derived from those forms of love that are proving especially useful in countering addictions.

The Three Internal States of Loving

All of the eight ways of loving are doing or action-filled behaviors. However, the actions of the three ways of loving presented in this chapter are achieved primarily by work on the inner self. This inner work involves attitudes, values, opinions and perceptions. Codependents often have been programmed to operate from fear-based internal states. For healthy, positive, love actions to flow, the codependent must work to change internal states blocking love to internal states promoting love.

How Do We Develop Intimate Love?

Affirmational Loving - ***You Really Are Special.*** Affirmational loving can best be defined as the series of acts that demonstrate emotional support, appreciating the one-of-a-kind (or unique) attributes of the loved one, showing respect for the loved one, and acting in a way that demonstrates the loved one is highly valued.

If I affirmationally love you, I spend time appreciatively listening to you. If I'm codependent, my listening is much more likely to be fear-based; that is, I listen for those things I fear or suspect may threaten the relationship.

If I'm codependent, when I hear you say, "I think I'll go visit my sister," I immediately, and often subconsciously, think things such as, "Is that safe? Is your sister for or against us? Are you really going there or are you going off to see someone else? Is this just a way to get away from me because you're losing interest in me? How can I use this to influence you my way? Does this mean I'm losing control of you? Should I manipulate the situation to prevent you from going? Should I go along to be sure I stay in control? Will I have to do something about this visit upon your return? Are you going to do something I'll have to take care of?" These codependent reactive thoughts are aimed at keeping me safe by controlling you, although it may seem I'm doing it just to keep you safe and okay.

If I listen to the same announcement with affirmational love, I simply feel good that you're going to do something you want to do. I may say something like, "Have a nice visit I'll enjoy hearing about it when you return." And I may be thinking, "That's nice" and "I'll be sharing something with you."

Codependent spouses listen in order to determine whether anything is happening that threatens not only their mate but also their position. Affirmational love focuses attention on the loved one's feelings. The person experiencing the affirmational love feels affirmed, which provides a sense of wanting to open up and share oneself with the affirming one.

Talking to a codependent becomes increasingly difficult. It is like talking to both a critical parent and a child whose feelings are too sensitive. Being told what should or shouldn't have been done, represents control via blame. Seeing that certain spoken things result in hurt or worried expressions represents control via guilt. Realizing that nearly everything said is scrutinized for its effects on the codependent and on the relationship, precludes confiding or sharing personal experiences.

Those relating with affirmational love are focused on just enjoying the way their partners dance the dance of being themselves, the way they sing their songs of thoughts and feelings, revealing their minds, hearts, and emotions. In affirmational love, the partners focus on what can be appreciated and shared and not what must be influenced, altered, or controlled. It's not an examination; it's a sharing experience.

In affirmational loving, partners encourage each other's projects, desires, "stuff." In codependency, they encourage only doing things they want done, things they can manage or influence, things that keep them safe; things that independently might help the other's individuality are discouraged.

Codependent sexuality and sexuality with affirmational love are different in a number of ways. Many people who suffer from codependency are quite externally dependent instead of internally or self-dependent about their sexuality. A codependent's sexuality is often sacrificed for the mate's approval. Codependency leads to directly, indirectly or even unconsciously communicated statements such as "I'll do anything you want sexually; abuse me, use me, just don't leave me."

As a therapist, I've heard these ruinous messages all too often in counseling. Sadly, it usually comes from a person who doesn't really enjoy sex. When they learn to healthfully realize their ability to delight in sex, dramatic changes occur and they start initiating sex play and saying what they like. They are honest and open, lovingly able to say things such as, "I'm so turned on just looking and listening to you that I really want you right now," a wonderfully loving affirmation. The focus changes from just pleasing you so you will feel okay toward me, to being able to sexually appreciate and affirm a partner's sexiness. In a very mated and personal way this follows the ancient wisdom conveyed in the admonition "to love others AS you love yourself."

In codependency, one loves oneself, only, if at all, after having completely loved another. In traditional, neurotic narcissism, one loves another only after thoroughly loving oneself, if ever. In healthy, real love, one often loves oneself as, not before or after, loving another. The result is that both partners get to be affirmed simultaneously. It's a very "I win, you win, nobody loses" way of helping each other be okay.

In codependency, there is little self-affirmation. Usually the codependent person practices self-sacrifice in order to get at least a little affirmational love from the person they are dependent upon. That person is too busy being dependent on something else like alcohol, power, parental approval, gambling, drugs, status, sex, or money to give anything but stingy or manipulative false affirmation.

The codependent probably was programmed to do this in childhood by parents who, because of their problems, were either stingy or manipulative with their affirmational love actions. Thus, the codependent got programmed to value love by someone who did not easily give real affirmational love. The codependent person avoids, discounts, or discards people who are good at affirming another's value and worth, and is instead attracted to their parent-surrogate who is poor at appreciating the value of others.

On the rare occasions when a codependent gets all the affirmational love needed from the person they are dependent on, they do what most offspring do. They leave their surrogate-parent mate and go off to start life on their own. Unless their mate also matures, making them both capable of adult-to-adult love, the relationship of a codependent is doomed to end or to stay a largely unloving one. It is highly unlikely that an addicted mate will have great proficiency in giving affirmational love. However, in CoRecovery work (especially, the system of teamwork), the growth of each spouse and the positive growth of the system itself can be coordinated. In this way, the addicted person can learn to love their mate instead of the addictive elements, and to base their renewed relationship on truly loving behaviors.

In affirmational love, there is a lot less seeking or giving advice. Each party respects the other's ability to figure out their personal situations. In codependency, there is often a lot of advice giving—whether it's sought or not—because advice affords a chance to control. In affirmational love, the tendency is to appreciate and honor the partner's work at self-control.

In affirmational love, a partner thinks, "I constantly enjoy your being in the process of your life; much as I see and appreciate a beautiful sunset, I see and appreciate you. With delight and honesty, I respect the awesome collection of miracles that you are, and I express this to you. I see and show my affirmation of your true worth as a person, independent of me as well as in my life."

In the CoRecovery program, we have made some remarkable breakthroughs in getting couples to take a look at their mate's uniqueness. The more you get to really know a mate, the more you can see how your mate thinks, feels, and acts differently than you and also every other person. They are truly one-of-a-kind. They will never be a copy of you or be exactly what you think they should be. This fact may scare, trouble, and worry people stuck in codependency. But the realization of uniqueness is a source of marvel and awe in real love. "If I love me enough and love you enough, I can really get pleasantly surprised by all the unique ways you are you."

With CoRecovery training, after much work we hear people say wonderful things such as, "For the first time I'm really seeing you, and you really are special." Or, "All this time I've never really seen you, and you're so wonderful just the way you are." Or, "You're so different than me and that's wonderful." Or, "When I see things through your mind it's all so unusual. It gives me a whole new way to see everything, and it's fantastic." Or, "I used to just try to get you to think like me. Now I see you have to think and feel everything your own way. What a stupid thing I've done in the past trying to control how you are you. If I had ever succeeded, I would have just made you a poor copy of me or the parent I wish I'd had. Keep being the unique, amazing you and I'll keep being the unique, amazing me, and we'll have two amazing worlds to share with each other."

These revelations provide a great sense of relief and often come with a lot of tears. It is a relief to finally see who's really there and not have to control him or her. It can end the essential loneliness that so many codependents feel. "When I don't have to be in charge of you, when I can let you do that and let you be the primary changer in your own life, I get to see and appreciate just who I'm really with."

In affirmational love, I tend to be your cheerleader, not your puppeteer, overseer, or controller, seldom even your coach. I let you do all that yourself. My actions, as well as my words, convey, "I'm on your side, I'm a keen supporter of you, and I believe in you and your worth. I'm not looking to alter the basic you although I cheer for your continued growth, development, potential, and healthfulness. If I see you being self-destructive, I'll affirmationally love you by emphasizing your worth more than the destructive behavior. I'll challenge you to reach your own potentials for health and well-being because I do believe in you."

In codependency, a person does the opposite of all this. Looking back, those who engaged in codependency and lost their mates because of addiction-related death often says something like, "I never really wanted Wendy to get treatment for her addiction because I was afraid she would get well and leave me."

I remember a severely codependent young woman who told how she actively opposed treatment for two husbands. The first died of an overdose; the second, drunken, in a car accident. She said she used to buy drugs and alcohol for them because they were pleased with her when she did that. Twice she had gone to bed with a dealer to get drugs for her first husband so he wouldn't be upset with her when she returned without the drugs. She was so dependent on her husband's approval that she helped him steal money from her parents. Finally, with a third man, in therapy she was learning to challenge him to work on his self-improvement because she now could affirm worth in both herself and him.

I also remember a highly codependent man who brought his diabetic wife sweets because it pleased her so; they felt close acting like conspiratorial naughty children together when he did. She almost died in a diabetic coma. They learned to see just how subtle and deadly their mutual codependency was. With work, they decided they could be like naughty, conspiring adolescents and have adventurous sex in all sorts of forbidden ways and places. This was a considerable improvement over their former behavior, allowing them to affirm natural and healthy sexuality and adventurousness in each other. They learned to respect each other's real safety issues.

Of course, these are relationship systems. The addicted mate helps to foster the codependent's behavior and then later resents it because he feels inadequate or guilty. The reassuring message is that codependents can learn how to change their codependent behaviors into truly loving behaviors. Codependents can understand the motivation behind some of their ineffective behaviors and then choose to substitute loving behaviors that succeed. They can start positive change in the relationship by changing their own behavior. Even if the addicted or recovering mate doesn't pick up on the change right away, the codependent can start to feel better because there is a healthy dose of self-love in all the behaviors of love, and believe me, healthy self-love feels a lot better than codependency. And if the couple is working on these changes together, it's more likely both will understand the counterproductive old patterns and see the benefits of substituting loving behavior systems.

Affirmational loving is about first noticing, then appreciating, and then conveying the value and worth that exists in the loved one. It is, in a sense, selfish in its origin. To notice and appreciate value is quite pleasurable for the one who does it; conveying affirmation is pleasing for the one who practices it.

When a couple learns mutual affirmation, they sense that something strong and powerful exists in their teamwork. Codependency usually results in a vague feeling that something weak and unhealthy is occurring. In CoRecovery the sense of "We are strong individually and yet so much stronger as a couple," is something CoRecovery couples come to use against their problems.

Moreover, according to several different research findings, affirmational loving is very important for survival under stress. For example, it was discovered in occupational sociology that men who lost jobs because factories closed experienced lower cholesterol, fewer illnesses, and significantly less depression, if they had emotionally supportive, affirming mates. Stress, illness, and depression were much higher in men who had no spouses and men who had less-affirming and less-emotionally supportive spouses (Gore 1978). Among pregnant women who had a great deal of stress in their lives, those who were measured as having affirmationally supportive loving experienced fewer complications than those not receiving such supportive, affirmational love (Nuckolls, Cassel & Kaplan 1972).

Clearly, the supportive function of affirmational love can be critical to our partner. Sometimes codependents are so involved in their individual survival that they actually withdraw support when their mate really needs it. Seeing a mate as sick, dying, in real danger, or failing in an important area can be so threatening to people deep in their codependency that they retreat to escape the threat.

I remember being called in to help a man with a life-threatening liver disease. The strange thing was his wife refused to see him in the hospital. She did come to see me. She quickly opened up explaining how she had tried to take care of her husband for years. She made sure he always had enough beer and cigarettes so he would be pleased with her, and stay home. She cried saying how she had lost him to that damn disease, that damn hospital, those damn doctors, and especially those damn nurses. With help she soon came to realize that seeing her husband under the influence of others meant a sense of loss of control and a sense of deep abandonment to her. These feelings were something she had been fighting ever since her father appeared to have lost interest in her when she was eleven. He had, she agonizingly remembered, "taken off with that damned other woman and her damned daughters." She did the necessary work to resolve these feelings, and then was able to visit her husband in the hospital. Before long she learned self-affirmational loving and that dissipated her fear of loosing her man to other women. Later, together, they developed new ways of affirming each other's worth and were able to have a number of healthier years together before he died. After his death she came to me with thanks for helping her to see that her fear of abandonment had almost resulted in her abandoning her husband when he needed her the most. She also said their last years were the best years because they both had learned to see what was truly special about each other—which is, of course, the essence of affirmational loving.

Self-Disclosure Loving - ***Thank You for Letting Me Know the Real You.*** The second major form of conveying love is called self-disclosure loving. It is often the form of loving that codependent people find most threatening, and the one they are usually most hesitant to honestly explore. Self-disclosure loving involves increasingly revealing what you really think, what you really feel, what you really do, what you have done, and want to do intimately with another.

Self-disclosure means taking the risk of going more and more psychologically naked with a loved one. That is a far more difficult form of nakedness than any other since the most intimate parts of a person are not physical but emotional. If I love you I risk letting you know who I really am. Moreover, because there is so much to know about each of us, and because we keep changing all the time, self-disclosure is a lifetime endeavor. We need daily, emotional weather reports on each other to remain current in our knowledge.

Codependency drives people to be in touch with only certain parts of their mate, and blind to others. As one codependent man said, "From my alcoholic mother, I learned how to be hypersensitive to female moods. If I could just keep aware of a woman's moods, especially my mother's, I could exert some influence and maybe even keep her from wanting to drink, or from being mad at me. Well, that's what I thought in regard to my alcoholic mother—now it governs how I think about my prescription addict wife. The trouble is, it is a burden trying to stay so aware. Also it makes me very afraid of disclosing my true feelings. You see, if I say the wrong things about myself, we could have a fight. And that would be followed by increased use of her favorite mood-altering substance, or she could use my self-disclosure against me. As a result, whenever I reveal even innocent, little things about myself, I feel really threatened."

This man trembled as he self-disclosed all this in his CoRecovery group in front of his wife. His wife, whom he had just talked about, hugged him—and with the therapist's help was able to simply, yet gently, say "I understand."

Then the trembling stopped.

Both came to know that their problems stemmed from childhood programming. Both saw that by disclosing these truths, and adding affirmational love, they were bonding in new, tender, yet strong ways.

A lack of self-disclosure adversely affects the sex lives of many codependents. Self-disclosure means getting in touch with what we want and revealing to each other what we like and dislike. It is hard to forget the case of a woman in a CoRecovery group who said, "I've been so busy taking care of your needs, I've just begun to become aware that I've got sexual wants too. In fact, I'm discovering I've got a lot of them."

Her husband said that no matter what she wanted, he would fight past whatever threat he felt and would help her with her desires.

She then said, "I want you to 'play rape' me for my pleasure—and do it just right." This was not an unusual desire; indeed, two other women in the group spontaneously shouted, "Yes" and "Right on."

Her husband said he felt really honored that she could disclose that, but added that he felt a lot of performance anxiety about doing it "just right." He also said his old defensive self wanted to get mad and blame her for being a slut, or something similar, so he wouldn't be threatened with having to "rape her just right." Three other husbands in the group said they also often tried to escape performance requirements by using attack defenses. Another said he used to feel that way, but that ever since he had discovered he and his wife could work through his making mistakes, everything was a lot more fun.

The woman who made the original self-disclosure suggested to her husband with a giggle that they go home and practice twenty or so times until they got it more or less right, earning her applause from most of the other women.

A week later they both reported they had experienced the most laughter-filled and silliest passion of their lives. They also said designing the "rape" together had been one of the emotionally closest and joyfully shared experiences of their entire relationship.

The husband confessed that as a result of the breakthroughs they had made through their "rape game," he had finally learned how his wife liked her clitoris to be rubbed. He had finally had the guts to ask her, and she finally showed him—after ten years of marriage.

Self-disclosing love behaviors are those acts and words that reveal the intimate facts and unique aspects of oneself, often at the risk of increased vulnerability. Sometimes what is revealed is not pleasant or enjoyable. A mate reveals an affair, a lie, or a betrayal. Such revelations risk rejection, disapproval or abandonment. The person hearing the self-disclosure has to make a choice. Will they let something be larger than love? Jealousy, insecurity, judgmentalism, one's sense of inadequacy all can be allowed to be bigger than love.

The question is, "Must I reject you to save myself from facing what you have done?" Or is my love of both me and you big enough to forgive? And is my love big enough to work with you, for us, to get past the unhappy revelation? In codependency, I can pretend to forgive anything just to hold on to you, but the secret rage inside me will eat away at me and at us. In codependency, I can internalize my anger and convert it to depression, which is an act of violence against myself. With real love, we can work to truly forgive and emotionally get over just about anything. Real love can forgive and go forward.

Once the primary things a person fears to tell about themselves are revealed, and the often hard work of acceptance is accomplished, a great union is usually achieved. As one client put it, "My lover forgave what I thought was unforgivable. That enabled me to forgive myself. In the future how could I ever not reveal and share myself with such a person? How could I not accept what my lover reveals to me? How could I not feel incredibly loved and loving to such a person?"

Self-disclosure creates a comfort few codependent people can ever know. Another client shared this with me, "I used to dance free-form by myself. One day after a session on self-disclosure I said to myself, 'Why not?' and I danced before my wife. She clapped, then she cried and said, 'Thank you, you're really letting me know the real you.' I was embarrassed but I felt real good, so I danced some more, and she started dancing too.

There we were dancing together for the first time without either one of us having to get high first. For us it was a great victory."

Self-disclosure involves letting someone know who you honestly are, your body, your thoughts, your emotions, and your behaviors. For a functioning couple, it involves repeatedly going psychologically naked with each other, even though that means exposing our personality quirks, embarrassing malformed or imperfect parts, our unhealed ugly wounds, and our disgusting scars from old traumas. To show these parts of your intimate, inner-self is a vulnerable and brave act, worthy of respect and returned self-disclosure. It enables us to get past our facade and become truly close. For it is only when we are naked with each other that all our various aspects can lovingly connect. So long as parts are not disclosed, we have parts not available for another's love. To adequately be an individual we often must pull apart, so as not to be enmeshed, and to know how we differ from others. Then, with what we discover about ourselves we can come together again, and share our new discoveries. Among those who love each other well, this creates a tide of flowing into ourselves and then back together to share what happened when we were emotionally away from each other.

Codependent people often need to be together all the time, fearing that their spouse won't come back, will do things they disapprove of when away, and won't share when they return. Codependents who feel this tend to pry, interrogate, and demand to know the private feelings, thoughts, and actions of their mates. They often do this overtly like a possessive, critical parent or covertly like a hurt child until they get the disclosures they are after. A stronger love helps a person invite the revelations of another, setting examples of self-disclosure. A more loving mate is interested in the whole of the loved one's experience. They are not just listening for transgressions or clues that might provide reassurance that, even while apart, their spouse lives in total compliance with their wishes.

To accept such elements in another without personal negation, rejection, or attack is a fine art. Sometimes this must be done in spite of difficult-to-handle reactions: "I'm insecure when you dance with another, so I'll work on that; and will you be supportive while I do this work on my insecurity?" is a question one lover in CoRecovery had for his mate. He also said, "I used to say, 'Don't you dare dance with anyone but me,' I was trying to fix me by controlling you. It just drove you away. Now I disclose my insecurity, ask for reassurance and my mate loves me more for it. What a difference!"

There are countless ways to self-disclose oneself to a mate. To uninhibitedly show your emotions is one of the best. Fear, joy, anger, serenity, boredom, ecstasy, sorrow, pride, and a thousand other variations of feelings constantly flow in us. To share these gives the gift of ourselves to our mates. Codependents often are attracted to mates who do not know the value of sharing. Men, in particular, are trained to suppress feelings, and therefore are often unable to share more than thoughts. Overcoming this is a major problem in many couples' relationships.

As one woman put it, "My father was an extremely unemotional, computer-type person who died from bleeding ulcers when I was 18. The physician said if he had learned to express his emotions it probably wouldn't have happened. By 19, I was married to someone just like my father. However, my husband has started getting into his suppressed, inner-child self and, wow, is he starting to be wild. It's scary, but I love it. Naturally, I hear a little voice in the back of my head trying to criticize him when he's not like my dad. I guess this happens when I think he's too much for me. Now I just reveal that the little voice is present, and we both say to that little person in my head, 'Shut up, it's going to be okay.'"

To reveal true thoughts, to explore moods together, to explore fears, hang-ups, shames, joys, naughtiness, and the childlike qualities that are in all of us, to let all this be known is so often what we hunger for. And it is what is so necessary for the growth of intimate mate love.

Like the other forms of love, self-disclosure love turns out to have some special healthy effects. At the University of New Mexico School of Medicine, it was discovered that patients with self-disclosing love relationships had significantly healthier immune systems, lower serum cholesterol, and better uric acid levels than those without such relationships (Thomas, Goodwin & Goodwin 1985). This means they exhibited healthier physical aspects than patients without self-disclosing relationships.

The healthfulness triggered by the behaviors of love is beginning to be increasingly understood—and so is the unhealthfulness of false love states, like codependency.

Tolerational Loving - *I'm Not Enough . . . YET.* Tolerational love is the name of the next major category of how humans show love. Tolerational love is defined as acts demonstrating an acceptance of the less-pleasant, but largely nondestructive, aspects of the loved one with nonjudgmental affect or emotion. In true, close, intimate contact a loved one will do things you don't like—do them repeatedly because it's part of a habit structure. Your beloved may be a morning person and you're a night person; may like large gatherings and you're a more one-on-one person; may like silly, laughter-filled sex and you like quiet, sweet, love making. In healthy love these and many other differences are tolerated. They may even come to be enjoyed as actions which endearingly represent your mate's unique way of being an individual.

Codependent mates usually have one of two problems with tolerational love. Quite common is the ruinous, passive codependent problem of over-tolerating the destructive behaviors of a loved one, especially the problems involving addictions. Sometimes in counseling sessions I hear a passive, codependent person say things like, "Even after your car wreck, your drinking was okay with me so long as it was okay with you. All that mattered to me was that you loved me. Anything else you did didn't bother me." With deeper work the person who says this sort of thing usually comes to say something like, "Now that I feel stronger I can express real love for you. Your health and well-being mean a lot to me. Before, it only mattered that you love me. Now I see that doesn't represent really loving you; it just represents being dependent on feeling loved by you."

One patient working at growing real love told her husband, "I was really awful. I used to over-tolerate everything you did—the drugs, the jobs you lost, all the ways you hurt yourself. In fact I even had a fantasy I'm ashamed to admit. I was so dependent on your seal of approval that I'd daydream of you telling me for hours how wonderful I was, and then you would go out and get killed in a car wreck, and I'd be sad but strangely relieved. If you died loving me, I'd never have to fear losing your love. Now I understand I didn't tell you I wanted you to stop your self-destructive habits out of this twisted fear. I would rather loose you to death in a state of loving me, than risk your disapproval and rejections. Now I want your well-being over my own insecurity, and that's real love."

This sort of emotional position is a kind of tolerance based on deficiency, not on love. Codependents can often look like they are lovingly tolerant of their mate's behaviors, or at least are long-suffering and accepting. In truth, they just don't focus much on their personal issues because being loved is more important than really loving. Sometimes this is well-hidden under a mask of solicitation and seemingly caring behavior. A man I once worked with very thoughtfully got his wife's prescriptions, helped with her chores, made sure she got enough rest, and did other ostensibly loving behaviors. The trouble was he also got her cigarettes, right up to the day she died of lung cancer. He later understood that his acts did not represent love as much as they represented appeasement. With regret he knew he had contributed to her death. In real tolerational love the goal is to tolerate the less-pleasant, nondestructive aspects of another and to deal in a tolerant pro-change style with the destructive aspects, not to live in denial or to be blind to their existence.

The second codependent problem with tolerational love is nearly opposite to tolerating too much. Highly controlling codependents can find it very difficult to overlook, to be truly lenient of, or to be flexible about a great many things. A dominant, codependent person often feels the need to manage almost everything about another's life. Hence, they tolerate very little. Again they can sound tolerant if they take a more covert approach. Their thinking process may be, "If you wear that sharp-looking dress to the office one of the guys there is sure to come on to you. He might be more attractive than me, and I could lose you to him." Instead they will say something like, "Gee, you look great in that dress, but don't you think it's just a bit too much for the office? You wouldn't want to make your supervisor think you're trying to outshine her, would you? Why don't you play it safe and switch to the gray suit?" Thus covert codependents behave in a way to ensure their individual safety, while seeming to act in their mate's best interest. The mate who experiences this, slowly develops a desire to get out from under this sort of influence, but often never realizes why. Such mates experience a set of vague, suffocated, never-quite-good-enough feelings. These feelings can undermine self-confidence and self-love development. Real tolerational love behaviors help the development of self-esteem and the growth of healthy self-love.

Overt codependents are often more blunt. They may just say something like, "That dress is too sexy for the office; take it off. What are you trying to do, seduce somebody there? Who are you trying to look so good for?" Of course all the mate's honest responses, explanations, facts, true reasons have no influence on this sort of codependent's intolerant insecurity. The problem concerns growing enough self-love. With enough self-love one is able to trust one's attractiveness to hold a loved one. Until this is accomplished the overt codependent will rely on overt jealous and possessive controlling actions. When codependents learn to love themselves sufficiently they will trust their worth as being enough to keep someone they love around.

The overt and the covert codependent, the dominant and the more passive seemingly overtolerant codependent, all need to develop true tolerational love abilities. Tolerational love is a key to breaking these destructive cycles.

When a couple works on developing healthy tolerational love styles together, they help each other confront some of their most important blocks to true, healthy self-love. Here are two examples of interactions that show how this can work.

"Lover, I'd really like you to be okay when I masturbate with my vibrator," one woman said to her husband in counseling. He was able to reply, "I guess I will probably be okay as soon as I believe enough in my own manhood." She was able to reassuringly add, "Have no fear of that. I see you as a very manly man. You're more of a strong, okay man to me when you are comfortable with what works for me. You're not one of those weak men who has to hide his insecurity behind acting tough and insisting that something is wrong with a woman if a man's not everything sexually to her."

This was said in a CoRecovery couple's group and all the women agreed and told this husband that they greatly admired his courage in being able to deal with this topic as he was doing. One of the other husbands was able to ask his wife if she could tolerate his masturbation, and she replied, "I guess I have to see that your masturbating is not a sign of my inadequacy. I always thought it meant that I'm not enough for you sexually. What I have to do is to tolerate me more to tolerate you more. If only I would just be okay with my own sexuality, I'd be okay with yours." It was not long before this lady and her husband were developing a much better sex life.

So much of tolerational love toward another has to do with how well we accept and tolerate our inadequacies, inconsistencies and our present lack of development. One of the best words to learn is "Yet" for developing tolerational love. "I'm not sexy enough" becomes, "I'm not sexy enough—YET!" Thus a sense of sad, stuck futility can turn into motivated hopeful action. "I'm not lovable" with "yet" added, can turn despair into dedicated learning about what it takes to grow more loveability.

One of the sadder things I hear in counseling goes something like this: "I used to hate his messiness, his socks and underwear on the floor, and his tools on the kitchen table. Now, I hate not seeing them there. The neatness just reminds me he's gone, and I miss him so. If only I'd been more accepting it might have helped, but I drove him off with all my bitching about every little thing that wasn't just perfect."

One of the most joyful things I hear in counseling sessions goes: "When I saw you could tolerate my failings, I started to accept that it was okay not to be perfect. Somehow that helped me want to be better and work on my shortcomings more. Your acceptance of me led to my acceptance of me, which led in turn to my doing a lot more to improve. Before I just felt guilty and futile. Thank you for loving me so well."

Some couples make a list of all the things they are intolerant of; then they start working on what that intolerance says about themselves, instead of what it says about their mate. "I'm intolerant of dirty dishes because I'm afraid my mother will drop by and criticize me for not being a good wife and mother. That's why I'm after you to wash every cup the minute you're through with it," said one woman in a burst of self-understanding about her intolerance.

Tolerational love is essential for keeping couples healthy and together. Intolerance is one of the most destructive factors in relationships. Research into intolerance revealed that an inability to feel healthy self-love, an inability to consistently show love to others, inability to feel secure, and inability to avoid being physically abusive all correlated highly with intolerance in individuals (Horton 1990). Such unresolved problems often make being healthfully mated virtually impossible. If intolerance is a strong feature of a relationship, seeking treatment is strongly recommended.

Many couples find great closeness and trust through love that shows tolerance. I recall a couple who were doing poorly at being emotionally intimate. She had a bisexual past, and he was raised within a church community that preached far more guilt and judgement than love and understanding. After deciding to center himself attitudinally in love and to come to his wife from this loving position, he was able to tenderly say, "The programs in my head from my past push me to judge you, but the real me only loves you." That was the beginning of true closeness for them.

I remember another couple who had a lot of trouble with affairs. She said, "I can tolerate my affairs because I know it doesn't mean anything, but I can't tolerate yours. You might fall for one of those women you bed and leave me." He said simply, "That's exactly how I feel." As they honestly explored their problem a simple pattern emerged. Both discovered they were having affairs to be able to tolerate their spouse's affairs. It became clear that theirs was one of those common, although hidden, feedback loop systems which couples slip into. "I have to have an affair to keep feeling okay about myself every time I find out you've been to bed with someone else," was something they both could say. With this out in the open, both were able to understand themselves and the stupid cycle they had gotten into. With the growth of tolerational love both felt support, and were able to make a new and successful pattern that replaced the old one.

The psychology of tolerational loving is apparently trickier than some of the other forms of demonstrating love and there are several parts to consider. These involve the externalization and internalization of intolerance. Intolerance definitely has its biological problems. The spouse who behaves with frequent or intense acts of intolerance and anger against their mate and others, tends to produce excessive amounts of a brain chemical known as norepinephrine. Over time this negatively effects their heart, helps to increase blood pressure and reduces cholesterol control. In excess, it seems to also damage the lining of the coronary arteries (Hamburg, Elliot & Parron 1982). Frequent occurrences of intolerant anger have also been linked to lower disease resistance (Miller 1986; Justice 1988).

The biological effects of internalized intolerance can also be severe. If on the outside we seem to be acting tolerantly, but instead we are "stuffing it" all down inside ourselves with conscious suppression or subconscious repression, the effects tend to be just as bad as externalized intolerant anger. In a sense this "stuff it" or "swallow it" psychological mechanism is a sort of false tolerance. It is also exactly what goes on in many codependent relationships. Because of this, codependency is a prescription for getting physically sick. Conversely, one of the many joys I have in treating codependent couples is seeing and hearing about their physical health improvements. As true tolerational loving increases, I often hear their physicians remark on the patients' recovery from various illnesses. One remark that I especially enjoy remembering was made about a codependent couple that seemed to catch every infection that came along. The physician said, "I don't see them anymore. There is too much love in their lives for them to get sick."

In true tolerational loving a person tends to do two negative things with positive results. First, they often do not let the external negative have an internal negative effect, like "water off a duck's back." Many people do not know how to do this. Recent expressions in our culture like "don't sweat the small stuff" point to people starting to learn this stress management approach. Healthy self-love and healthy couple love requires this. All too often in codependent couples one "flies off the handle at every little thing" and the other keeps acting tolerantly when, really, they are building up to an explosion of anger or an implosion of depression. True tolerance is not occurring and both are increasing their likelihood of getting physically sick.

Healthy love-functional couples can and do learn a teamwork based on the concept that stress control has more to do with not letting stressors distress you than with escaping stressors. Tolerational loving can be a great assistance in this health maintenance action. Going to the trouble to jointly learn about stress management is often a very good couple's growth activity.

The next factor in tolerational loving has to do with healthy catharsis of what stressors do "get in." Psychological catharsis means about the same thing as "blowing off steam" or "getting it out of your system." This can be done destructively or constructively. Healthy love-functional couples learn to do it constructively; codependent couples do not. The physical health benefits of constructive emotional catharsis and other factors related to tolerational loving are increasingly being discovered (Locke 1986). Healthy tolerational love can allow for a mate's need to "blow off steam" or purge stress, so long as it is done without attacking people or damaging anything important. Griping about conditions, crying, "cussing at the wind" and all sorts of tension release mechanisms can be tolerated without fear, or the need for defensiveness. This constitutes constructive release of that which might seem intolerable if it was not purged. Attacking a person verbally or physically or breaking things is destructive and is not acceptable behavior in love-functional couples. As a couple works toward healthy, tolerational loving they learn to neither internalize or destructively release their negative feelings. This means a balance occurs which shows up in their physical as well as their emotional health.

We have discussed the three ways of loving that focus more on internal work—affirmational, self-disclosure and tolerational loving. Now we continue to the ways of loving that focus more on outward, physical manifestations.

CoRecovery . . . 6

How Do We Make Love Really Show?

In contrast to the three ways of loving that involve an inner focus, the next four concern things you do; actions that can be more easily perceived by others. The four ways of making your love show require a positive, willing, inner attitude to inspire them, however. If this positive attitude is weak or missing, you may need to do some inner work to overcome psychological obstacles.

Expressional Loving - The Looks and Sounds of Love

Expressional-loving behaviors are among the most basic and most quickly delivered forms of showing love. Expressional love involves sending love through tones of voice, gestures, postures and facial expressions. Most people are surprised to learn that, according to communication researchers, in personal, face-to-face, direct communication only seven percent of the communication is through the words being spoken. Approximately thirty-five percent is in the tonal variations of the voice. I can say "I Love You" in a matter-of-fact way, or bored, or enthusiastically, or tenderly or even with hostile cynicism. My words are the same in each case but my tones can convey the real meaning. Approximately fifty-five percent of personal communication is relayed by our movements. If I say "I Love You" with a frown or a shrug, it communicates an entirely different message than if I say it with a smile and my arms flung wide open to you. If I say "I Love You" as I lean away from you, you may interpret it as emotionally distancing myself. But if instead I lean toward you, your interpretation may be exactly the opposite. The movement of a hand, a raised eyebrow, a slightly bowed back, a wide-eyed glance, a shoulder turning away, sitting closer than usual, a softer tone, a sharp edge in the voice, a touch of a whisper, each of these is perceived and interpreted subconsciously if not consciously. Some research in human communication shows that unconsciously we are interpreting about 300 bits of expressional or nonverbal information per minute in normal face-to-face conversation (Burgess 1985).

Understanding this helps to explain why after World War II, thousands of American GI's married thousands of Japanese women with neither knowing each other's verbal languages. They communicated quite well expressionally. Literally, it is not what is said but the way it is said that makes the difference.

Love can be conveyed to us by soft, caring sounds even before we are born, according to pediatric and developmental research. Very soon after we are born, smiles and voice tones conveying love change our neurochemical balances for the better. The lack of these positive, loving behaviors often disturb the digestion and sleep of infants even though nothing else is wrong. Throughout life the sounds and looks of love influence us in very important ways.

Dr. R. M. Nerem and Associates investigated some of the factors related to expressional love and reproduced with laboratory animals what previously had been discovered with humans. Rabbits on fat-intensive diets who were lovingly talked to developed significantly lower rates of atherosclerosis than a comparison group of rabbits on the same diet receiving only routine laboratory treatment (1980). Neuroanatomist, Marian Diamond of the University of California at Berkley, found that other lab animals responded to tender, loving sounds by living considerably longer and their cerebral cortexes were consistently larger (better brain development) than lab animals not lovingly addressed (Hopson 1984).

Dr. B. O'Regan at the New York Institute for the Advancement of Health reviewed the emerging research on positive feelings. Dr. O'Regan concluded that the evidence suggested that smiling resets the automatic nervous system in a way that makes it less reactive to stress (1985). These are just a few examples of how research is discovering the importance of expressional love factors.

It is unfortunate that in codependency the expressional communication of many people is distorted especially as it relates to expressions of love. Codependency contains a strong element of underlying anxiety. This anxiety usually comes from being insufficiently or inappropriately loved; that results in the fear a loved one will abandon the codependent, and they will return to being unloved or at least poorly loved. Since codependents are poor at healthy self-love, they quite accurately feel they cannot take care of themselves emotionally. This leads to fear-based facial expression, tones of voice, gestures and postures of two basic types. One is fear hidden behind happy, loving, kind, friendly looks and sounds. The other is fear hidden behind authoritative, strong, indifferent or domineering looks and sounds. Both types of expressional language try to manipulate for the communicator's safety rather than for demonstrating love. Happy, positive looks and sounds in a codependent convey "be happy with me and I'll be safe." Indifferent and domineering expressions say "be afraid of me, and I'll be safe." Both systems are rooted in the codependent's early family and societal deficiencies in demonstrating love.

Some societies are quite good at teaching kids to expressionally show love and others are not. In his excellent analysis of love-based cultures and hate-based cultures, Dr. Rubin Fine, Director of the New York Center for Psychoanalytic Training, found some cultural groups so good at expressing love that virtually no cases of murder, arson, severe physical assault or sex crime exist. The Hutterites of the Rocky Mountain area of Canada have had no such crimes since 1875. The Ifaluk of Micronesia, the Tasaday of the Philippines, and the Mountain Arapesh of New Guinea all are cultures with high incidence of love expression and come close to being violence- and crime-free. Many of the illnesses, both physical and emotional, thought to be related to a lack of love are virtually nonexistent in these cultures. Conversely in the hate-based cultures the frequent and easy expressions of love are inhibited or restricted to rare situations. In such cultures the systematic, violent killing of women, children, the weak, and infirm has received cultural support, or at best indifference. Nazi Germany, both the Tauade and the Dobu of New Guinea, and the Jivaro of Ecuador all have extolled antilove behaviors as virtues. In doing so they rendered and experienced great violence, slaughter, and crime. They also exhibited high incidence of stress illness. All these hate-centered cultures have been destroyed or reformed by contact with less hate-centered cultures (Fine 1985).

Our western world is in a great cultural battle as to whether or not we will be a hate-based, an indifference-based or a love-based society. The archetypical, highly expressive Italian, the fervent Israeli, the animated Irish, the dancing Greek and the passionate Latin are far healthier models than the archetypes presented by the image of the strong, silent American, the severe Prussian, the stoic Scandinavian, or the aloof, upper-class Englishman.

Couples in CoRecovery groups typically have a lot of work to do to get their sounds and looks to genuinely express love. Breaking out of cultural and subcultural training is often hard work. "You never look like you love me," one woman screamed at her Minnesota-raised, former Lutheran minister, husband. At first, he blandly replied that he did not think it was appropriate for him to have different looks. "I'm going out with the first man I can find that knows how to show a tender loving look if you don't learn how," was her reply. Tears began to form in his eyes and his jaw quivered, and he said in a choked voice, "I don't know how. Oh, please show me how; somebody show me how!" "You're doing it now. You're looking real human, not like a stone face," his wife said. With coaching and feedback he tried on for size many facial expressions that night. As he did so, he had to pay the price of feeling awkward, embarrassed and foolish. But at the end of the evening he said it felt like a plaster cast his face was imprisoned in had finally broken. His face never looked the same again. An interesting affirmation of this change happened a week later. A security guard at the top secret defense plant he where worked thought he was an imposter because he just did not look the same. He relishes telling that his fingerprints had to be compared to those on record for him to get in that day.

Sometimes men, especially, have to do extra work to let their tones of voice and faces show love. We live in a culture that shows us "heroes" who kill without a change of expression. In some places we still proclaim the strong silent type as admirable. Our society has little modeling of sweet and tender looks and sounds by male role models. In such a society it's difficult for males to learn enough about expressional love. In CoRecovery groups one guy typically is working on a problem of expressional communication. With practice he gets some praise from the females for some of his tones or gestures, or facial expressions. He then shows the other guys and they copy him, sometimes sheepishly. By learning to purposely link his face, gestures, postures and tones to his true inner feelings, he learns to show expressionally that he loves his lady. Typically he is surprised that he's feeling a lot more and is more aware of what he's feeling. More than one guy in this process has proclaimed, "I'm alive, I'm alive, I'm feeling so much!" Typically their mates feel joy and say something like, "I knew you could do it." It's a beautiful process to watch a guy show his feelings for the first time in years and to see the closeness it brings to a couple.

Most men with a lot of 'macho' training initially resist help. When the other men in a group challenge them and the women encourage them they start giving it a try. After that there is seldom any great desire to return to the stone face, the false smile mask, or the power look so many codependent men wear to keep themselves safe.

Many codependent women have to get past an elaborate set of false looks and sounds to get really good at expressional love. When following cultural or family training some women specialize in various false smiles to hide their real anger, fear or manipulations. Others specialize in sheepish, childlike, innocent looks and sounds to manipulate their men. One man said he came home unexpectedly and entered from a side door, unintentionally going unnoticed. He was surprised to hear his wife and two daughters sounding happy, strong, outgoing and definitely confident as they talked with each other. He listened for quite a while and then entered the room they were in. As he told it, upon hearing him approach, they immediately switched their tones to whinny, wimpish and needy, each wheedling him for some favor or advantage. "This is what I got for playing big powerful daddy and working to keep them dependent on me, instead of helping them to become self-reliant," he said.

Most of us don't spend much time thinking about what our voice is communicating, what messages our body language is sending, or what our face is telling people about how we feel. An exercise we sometimes do in CoRecovery groups is to have one person slowly say the alphabet. To every letter said the listener has to respond with a different facial and gesture expression, as if they were experiencing a different emotion with each letter. Delight, serenity, anguish, awe, conspiratorial intimacy, sexual desire, pride, sorrow, anger, anxiety, victory, surprise, silliness, tenderness, sweetness, kindness, joy and many other feelings can all be said nonverbally to a person while they talk. This is a part of learning to listen with love.

In loving listening we expressionally communicate while we listen to another verbally communicate. The old "I hear you, why do I have to look at you" doesn't do it. We often hear more with our eyes than with our ears. Remember fifty-five percent of personal communication is in what you see in the speaker's facial, body and gestural movements. Helping couples face each other, make and keep good eye contact (which is surprisingly difficult for codependents, who prefer to use lots of quick glances) and notice expressional language, are core training for couples who are out of touch emotionally with each other. There is often an embarrassment price to pay before this works, but once it does, it is wonderful to see the results. Real closeness, intimate showing and feeling of shared love get easy once a couple learns to improve their expressional love teamwork in communications.

"You used to flash such sexy looks at me. It turned me on every time. Then we moved in together and you haven't since. What's the problem, lover?" one mate asked. The answer was, "I never saw my folks do it. I never saw married people on TV or in the movies do it, so I guess subconsciously I thought once we started acting married that premarried behavior had to go. I miss seeing you light up, so I guess I'll reactivate the sexy, flirtatious me." Then came one of the most provocative looks seen in a long time and boy, did her lover "light up" in response. From then on this couple was on their way back to the sexy love life they had once enjoyed.

The importance of being able to show genuine looks of love, the importance of being able to demonstrate the many emotions of love in voice tones, the importance of open-arm gestures, moving toward someone when they need love, all these expressional ways of showing love cannot be overstated.

A very Mississippi-raised lady was so glad to hear her Colorado, cattleman-husband eventually say, "Now I believe you; now you finally don't sound like you're trying to manipulate me." She had worked hard to get past her considerable training in traditional, coquettish "handling of men," as she called it. Long after she had given up manipulating men and become genuine, she still sounded devious, although now cute and sexy. Her very up front, straight-forward husband also had to learn to show his very real love feelings with tender, kind tones. To hear him able to whisper "I love you" with gentleness in his voice was inspiring. To hear her simply, and with womanly strength, reply how she felt his love and felt love for him was intimately awesome. Such can be the effect of expressional love.

Verbal Loving - *Now I Understand You.*

In regard to verbal love it is good to remember that love works like food. Many times in counseling I have heard something like, "Why do I have to tell her I love her, doesn't she know that by now?" Then I ask a rhetorical question, "So you think words are only to be used for conveying information?" Or I might metaphorically say, "That's like saying I fed you last year, why are you hungry this year?" Sincerely saying "I love you" and all other words conveying love is like serving a person a nourishing meal. Remember, people do well to eat several times a day.

Verbal love is defined as the behavior of verbally conveying words, pet names and phrases expressing love. Saying "I love you" aloud, frequently, honestly, and directly, is seldom a mistake. It can help your loved one know you're in touch with your love feelings for them at that moment. It can also help them in the all important, repeated, reexperiencing of love. Simple, honest things like, "I'm glad to see you, I respect you, I enjoy you, I'm glad you're in my life, you are very special to me," directly convey love.

Often therapists and counselors hear codependents say, "In my family I never heard 'I love you';" or, "To this day my father can't say he loves me;" or, "My mother died before we got to say we loved each other." We also hear, "My mom finally broke down and admitted she loves me. It meant so much;" or, "Since we started telling each other daily of our love, we've both been more calm and less stressed."

Many people, often the mates of codependents, express a discomfort with learning to say words of love. Many are embarrassed; some are suspicious of such expressions; others confuse words of love with something sexual. Usually these same people are also uncomfortable with close, deep intimacy. They want their mates to "just know" how they feel without learning to accurately express their love. Frequently they were raised to depend on indirect rather than direct ways of showing love.

Common expressions made by people not yet good at directly showing love are: "I come home, don't I?" "I clean your clothes and feed you." "I have sex with you." "I give you my paycheck, so doesn't that tell you I love you enough?" "Don't actions speak louder than words?" Direct and indirect communication of love are important. Both actions and words are needed. Although words are only seven percent of a personal communication, they provide accuracy, artfulness, judiciousness, comprehension and adroit ways of conveying love, as nothing else can.

Special phrases and pet names help a couple develop unique rituals that when heard will automatically stimulate feelings of their solid love bonding. "Whenever we say 'Stuttgart' to one another, we remind each other we got through one of the hardest times in our lives, and by comparison, whatever we are facing now will look easy compared to that," one military couple related. "Every time I privately get to call him my 'Pussy Pumper' I feel so happy and special, and he usually tells me the most wonderful, naughty things we're going to do together—it's all so lover confidential and sexy chummy, I just adore it," said one lady relating her newly developed way of communicating pet names with her spouse.

Codependent couples block and clutter their love communications with talk from five major problem areas. These five problem areas stem from what many authorities believe to be the core symptoms of codependency. Pia Mellody, one of the pioneers in codependency treatment, discusses these symptoms in detail as they apply to individuals (Mellody, Miller & Miller 1989). Here we discuss them as they apply to couples:

The first of these is the difficulty codependents experience because of their low self-love and consequent low self-esteem. Thus, when told they are loved, special, precious, or cherished, most codependent people make some self-effacing statement, tell of being inept at something, discount themselves, or start effusively telling their mate how he or she is loved. A subgroup may hide from the expression of love coming their way by bringing up problems, making jokes, changing the subject, mysteriously being silent, or pretending to be arrogantly and grandiosely aware they are wonderful. None of this helps them really get in touch with what is being said or how to respond, and honestly and accurately express their feelings.

Hungry for love, many codependent people will say "I love you," followed by a little, silent pause. This means they have not really said "I love you." Instead, they subtly have said, "Please tell me you love me." Sensing this many people do say, "I love you too" in reply but without much enthusiasm. The ever-aware, sensitive, codependent person picks up on the hollowness of the words, and feels once again that they are not truly loved or even lovable. This self-defeating setup is common talk of codependent couples. Out of this little interaction can come hurt, anger and anxiety which may dominate the next several hours of the couple's interaction.

"I love you, but I'm not worth much, so I won't tell you, because I see my words don't mean much to you" describes another attitudinal position many codependents take. This attitude inhibits their verbal expression of love. Others overdo saying words of love trying desperately to get their mates to be more verbally expressive of love. A constant barrage of honey, sweetheart, darling, delight-of-my-life, peaches, lover can overwhelm a mate and inhibit their expressions of endearment.

Sometimes it is surprisingly difficult helping codependents say "I love you" out loud, as a true expression of their love feelings, and not as a manipulation. Codependent couples need to get in touch with the fact that their love for one another is highly valuable and worth stating. With this awareness and with practice verbal loving can enhance coupleness.

A second major difficulty codependents have is verbally expressing the reality of their love for another moderately. Accuracy often demands moderation. Like children, many codependents express themselves either not at all, or in extremes. "You are absolutely the total, most wonderful person in all the history of the entire human race," is not a believable statement. "I find I'm growing increasingly fond of you" might mean more in adult-to-adult speech. Helping couples verbally express their love accurately, with artfulness and discrimination, leads to stronger and more lasting bonding experiences.

A third major problem blocking a codependent couple's verbal expression of love is their inability to ask, openly and directly, for what they want. One way I can verbally show you I love you is to tell you that you are the special person whom I desire, and I find you are able to help me satisfy my wants and meet my needs. As one sailor put it to his lover, "For me, baby, you got just what it takes, like nobody else I ever met." She felt very special on hearing this and said so.

Telling you my wants helps you know you are special to me because it is self-disclosure loving. Helping codependently distressed couples to start identifying their real love wants, their desires for affection, their sexual wishes, and their fun, pleasure proclivities and then to state them clearly is a major task in CoRecovery work. It honors a person to say that they are desired, and that there are certain things you wish to do only with them. Among codependent couples revealing wants is often hard. To them it sounds selfish and risks rejection.

This problem means a codependent's spouse has the impossible burden of guessing what their mate wants, trying to read subtle and contradictory hints, looking for hidden signs of what's really desired, and getting totally frustrated with all the unclear communications. It is a real gift of love to tell a spouse exactly and clearly what you want, how and when, and how much. It must have been a codependent who first said, "You must not really love me if I have to tell you what I need," and "Telling you what I want spoils it." Many a divorce has resulted from such thinking.

Getting and giving clear messages for good teamwork in sex is especially loving for many couples. Learning just nine words can completely reverse a deteriorating sex life for some people. The words are "up, down, right, left, harder, softer, faster, slower and good." "A little to the right, now softer and faster please, down just a bit . . . oh good-good-GOOD!!!" is just the type of thing many a couple needs to accurately communicate.

Questions like, "Which movie do you want to see?" "What restaurant interests you today?" can help lovingly share the burden of decisions. The usual codependent response, "Whatever you want, dear" is no help at all. "Lover, I want Chinese. Tell me what you want and we'll flip a coin and see which it will be tonight," was the way one couple learned to lovingly talk about these sometimes troublesome choices.

Related to this is the codependent's fourth problem, knowing and owning their reality. Many codependent people have been conditioned to be unaware of their feelings. They wait for someone else to tell them what to think, feel and believe. They have learned to live in reaction to another, rather than by their inner, natural guidance systems of emotions and desires. Thus they often say whatever they think their mate wants to hear, and think that is what they must feel or believe. Once in a CoRecovery group session, a very codependently conditioned man said to his mate, "I know after all these years it's going to come as a surprise to you, and please don't take it as an affront, but I don't think I really like anal intercourse. In fact, maybe I never liked it, although I know I told you I did over and over. I suspect now I made myself believe that, because you seemed to like it so much." This lack of being in touch with one's personal reality makes verbal expressions of love quite untrustworthy. A lot of work has to be done to get real feelings clearly and accurately known and then expressed. The benefits of this work, however, are clearly rewarding.

The above example also illustrates the fifth problem many codependents have. It's hard for a person programmed in codependency to set functional boundaries and express them to a spouse. "It's okay to talk to me all night, even though I have to get up at five in the morning and work a double shift," said one nurse to the husband she felt so dependent on. Later she learned to say more real, loving messages like, "I'm going to sleep now, and I'll be able to listen better tomorrow after I get some rest." Her husband understood and, because she stated parameters without rancor, he was able to feel loved by this honest sharing of her limits or boundaries.

In a CoRecovery group another husband told how he had discovered that his compliant, sacrificing wife had gone to sleep during intercourse because she wouldn't take care of her needs and say, "I'm too tired." At the time he took it as a great insult, but now he saw it as evidence of how his wife did not know how to set boundaries.

I love you partly by verbally sharing my inner feelings with you. This includes sharing my feelings that guide me to say things like, "Stop, that's too much for me," "I need this or that before I feel comfortable enough to help you with what you want." Feeling selfish or guilty, codependents are afraid to verbally share this kind of information. Many codependent people are out of touch with their personal emotional guidance systems. They must first do a lot of work to get in touch with these boundary-keeping feelings so they can be verbalized. Spouses in good teamwork can often help each other tune in to feelings that have previously gone unnoticed. It's a verbal act of love to genuinely and gently ask your mate, "What are you feeling?" and, of course, patiently listen as they explore deeply within themselves to find out.

Verbal love also has some very healthy effects on our bodies. Drs. Siegman and Feldstein when investigating the treatment of heart disease found that speaking slow, soft, positive loving words brought heart rates down (1985). Williams found that enthusiastic, positive talk of a loving, happy sort seemed to protect against the risk of heart disease (1985). Psychologists Ellen Langer of Harvard and Judith Rodin of Yale were able to relate positive, loving verbalization to significant improvements in stress hormone levels and the reduction of physical illness symptoms (1976). Clearly the evidence suggests verbalizations of love can and do make a very real difference in the lives of many.

Couples who are winning their battle against codependency are couples who go to the trouble to invent and practice new ways of behaving. To improve verbal love many couples make a list of a dozen or more things they would like to hear from their mates. They write the exact words, sentences, phrases, and terms of endearment they wish to hear. They exchange lists and practice saying the expressions lovingly. Many couples at first say they feel awkward, embarrassed, silly, or phony in both saying and hearing words of love. For some people words of love at first only trigger sexual feelings, for others a sense of being manipulated or trapped, and for others nothing at all.

Two concepts are useful in overcoming initial resistance. First, "If you stick with old ways of behaving, old results are all you're likely to get." If you want new results you have to pay the embarrassment price and do new behaviors. Old actions get old results, new actions get new results. The new behaviors feel strange and odd just because they are new. With practice they will feel fine, and they will usually get much better results.

The second concept simply put is, "Fake it till you make it." A very love starved man, after prompting, started mundanely saying "sweetheart" and "darling" to his equally love starved mate. She said, "It sort of makes me feel good to hear you say those words, even though I know you're reluctant to use them." He replied, "I'm glad you understand. That makes me want to say them more." Then he repeated the endearments with a little more sincerity. She started smiling. He looked at her closely and said, "My God, you really are my Darling and Sweetheart, and this is the first time in a long time I've let myself really feel that." They reached across to each other and hugged. Such can be the power of a spoken word of love.

Many who use the "Fake it till you make it" plan have to also understand and work past their programming in reluctance. Most do not experience immediate results and give up too soon. Many codependents have to get past their tendency to excuse and defend their less verbal spouses. "I don't want him to feel uncomfortable." "He doesn't have to tell me he loves me. I can just know it," and all the other excuses codependents make for their mates have to go.

The ancient admonition, "Love others as you love yourself" applies here too. As one stronger-than-she-used-to-be lady put it, "If you learn to sincerely enjoy telling me that you love me, you'll have a happy lady on your hands and if you don't, you won't!" Her all-too-often-silent husband got the message and with a long string of words said, "Baby, if that's what it takes to make my sweetheart, darling woman happy, then lover lady, you've got it in spades with ice cream on it." She laughed and looked delighted. He occasionally slipped back to his nonverbal habits but, from then on, it just took a little request from her and they were back to a lot of happy, playful, enriching verbal loving.

Tactile Loving - *It's the One I Love Touching Me.*

Tactile love is defined as physical contact demonstrating loving affection and loving sexuality. Touching, with love, someone you love is perhaps the most basic and consequential way to show love. Without loving touch infants who are otherwise cared for die of a disease known as *marasmus*. Before loving, holding, cuddling, and stroking became a part of the care program given to infant orphans, one hundred percent died before reaching the age of two in the institutions Dr. Henry Chapin studied. They died due to marasmus, a failure-to-thrive disorder, in which medications did little good without the inclusion of being held lovingly (1915). The pioneering work of Drs. Henry Chapin (1915), J. Brennemann (1932), Ruth and Harry Bakwin (1942), Rene Spitz (1947), R. Fried and M. F. Mayer (1948) and a host of others in pediatric research brought these facts to light in the first half of the Twentieth Century. Dr. Harry Harlow, the famous psychologist, later replicated this finding in the laboratory with monkeys (1965). Significantly, his book on this primate research is called *Learning to Love* (1971). Since then a great deal more has been discovered about the body's healthful reaction to loving touch. Whole books have been published about the research and the importance of tactile love. Let us just mention one finding in particular.

The world famous neuroanatomist, Marian Diamond, spent over 30 years studying what factors effect the brain and nervous system beneficially. She found that caregiving, holding, and stroking in tender ways were some of the most important influences on a brain's healthful functioning. Loving touch definitely resulted in enhancing both the health and longevity of the lab animals studied. Dr. Diamond then discovered corollary results in humans. Loving touch even aided brain growth in the elderly, something heretofore thought impossible (1983). Researchers discovered that those who get insufficient loving touch experience much slower healing of wounded tissue, greater likelihood of brain chemistry imbalances resulting in depression, anxiety, various forms of mental and emotional breakdown, and greater likelihood of substance abuse and addiction. Clearly loving touch is incredibly important.

Unfortunately, couples who have codependency problems frequently have problems with touch. These problems are of several types. The most severe are experienced by people who grew up in dysfunctional families where physical abuse happened in one or more forms. The dysfunctional alcoholic parent who, when drunk, strikes a child one night and sexually molests them the next, is an example. Typically, such parents lovingly hold and stroke when they are sober and then they begin to suffocatingly hold and touch as they start drinking again. This usually produces a very touch-confused adult. Some adult children of alcoholics subconsciously seek to be hit because hitting came before, or in the middle of, being lovingly attended to. Some seek insatiable sex because sex was a part of the only loving touch they received. Others are touch phobic and suspect all touch of being harmful, manipulative, controlling and a precursor to harm. Some who grew up in unloving, cold, untouching families seek touch of every kind to make up for the early deficits. Others who were taught that all touch is sexual turn every touch into a sexual occurrence. Still others who were taught that all sexuality is evil, feel guilt and shame with most touch, especially during or after sexual experiences. Many are hypersensitive and overreact to even the possibility of a touch. Milder, nonetheless serious and harmful, versions of this occur in people who grew up overly influenced by socially dysfunctional communities. A violent neighborhood, a physically abusive school environment, a guilt-and-shame oriented church and other units of our society can be dysfunctional. They can program a child in ways that later block the free and necessary flow of love, especially love via touch.

All too often a desperately touch-hungry codependent marries a touch-phobic spouse who only makes physical contact through sex or violence. This marriage choice, of course, comes from the programming in the computer-like part of the subconscious. This programming works to help people find someone with whom to reenact unresolved childhood conflicts in an attempt to finally put those conflicts to rest.

In CoRecovery groups and joint couple sessions I have been fortunate to see even the worst of such conflicts healthfully resolved. I recall a man who was repeatedly and violently sexually molested by both his alcoholic mother and his guilt- and sex-conflicted preacher-father. In adulthood he desperately sought, and then fled from, love. After marrying a very timid, unassertive, child-like woman with whom he felt safe, he discovered he could not bear to touch her. For three years he did no more than hold her hand, and, in typical codependent fashion, she blamed herself for his behavior. She came from an exceedingly nontouching family. Today they enjoy a rich life of love including more than enough tactile love to make up for their early childhood deficiencies. How did they get over such hard early conditioning? Well, it took quite a bit longer than usual, but they did it the same way most couples do in CoRecovery work.

First, they fearfully but lovingly decided to work as a team together fighting the problem and not fighting each other. After revealing their backgrounds to each other, they approached the problem of touch. He was instructed to rub her shoulders while she sat upright, fully clothed in a chair. As instructed he kept repeating out loud, "This is the body of the woman I love, and because it is a part of her, I will cherish it and touch it with tender love." He trembled but he was okay. However, on changing places, and as she began to touch him, he shook violently. She softly repeated the same sort of words. He replied, "It's the woman I love touching me with love, tender, precious, safe love for me." Slowly he calmed. Hand and foot rubs came later, and then touching the whole, yet clothed, back, arms and, with great difficulty, legs. They repeated this at home. Before long he could say touching each other was starting to feel nice.

Less clothing was hard, but at home this couple slowly, lovingly became able to touch with less and less on. Four sessions with male and four with female registered massage therapists taught them as a couple a host of nonsexual ways to touch each other. They practiced these at home.

There were setbacks. Nudity, nipple, buttocks, and genital touch fears were only slowly overcome. Eventually, this couple was able to make a whole new set of connections between touch and emotions, this time "good" emotions.

When this touch-traumatized man first joined a CoRecovery group he wouldn't let anyone hug him. All of us in the group knew he had really overcome his severe antitouch training when he sheepishly asked to try hugging and being hugged by the other group members. His wife cried deep sobs of joy for him, for she knew better than anyone how far he had come and what a great victory this was for him. Several couples in the group who also had hang-ups with touch were inspired to defeat their problems. Everyone agreed that if this couple could, as a team, defeat such severe antitouch programming, anyone could, with the right kind of retraining.

Another type of touch problem comes with the codependents who can't set boundaries for themselves. They allow any type of touch, having been trained to think they must sacrifice themselves to others. To love themselves they have to learn how to ask for what they do want and assert what they don't want. A very codependent female complained that sex with her husband was essentially like repeated rape experiences. She had been raped and said her assailant was less cold and rough with her than was her husband. He was astonished and very defensive when he first heard this. Then he learned to recenter himself in his love for her rather than to center in defensiveness. After that he was able to make a significant agreement. For a month he would only touch her where, when and how she wanted. Slowly as she learned to lovingly assert her wants, she and he together explored what might be pleasurable to her. With each tender, loving, careful exploration both discovered pleasures they had not known before. His old, cold, brutal sexuality gave way to the most care-filled ways of touching which included loving sexuality.

Much tactile love has little or nothing to do with sex. Touching to comfort, to share joy, to feel close, to be special together, and for a myriad of other reasons are very important for couples to learn, if they are going to do tactile love well. Lots of men have very poor training in the variety of loving touch. I remember a super-macho trained fellow who, upon returning from his first visit to Europe said, "They're all either homosexual or sex crazed over there because they're always touching each other—men with men, women with women, even old people." A man in the group who had been raised in Italy said, "No, it's you Americans who are afraid to show your friends any real love." It took a while but Mr. "Super Macho" learned that loving touch without getting carried away sexually was a good thing.

One of the most "touching" stories of tactile love I know came from an elderly gentlemen who belatedly learned that his sister was dying of a very painful and terminal illness. When he arrived at her bedside and held her hand she became calm. She came out of a medication-induced stupor and said she wanted to die but was afraid to, even though she was in extreme agony. She asked her brother to come very close and hold her. He did. Then she whispered, "I can go now," and passed away in his arms.

Such seems to be the power of loving touch.

Tangible Gift Loving - ***You Went Out of Your Way for Me.***

Tangible gift love is defined as acts of presenting tangible or financial gifts which represent the high, positive regard of love. Giving money and objects can, like all other behaviors of love be misused, overdone, or inappropriately accomplished. Done properly such gifts can often be an excellent form of showing love.

What really works in gifting someone is often surprising. A single rose can mean more than a dozen. The handmade object can be more touching than a highly crafted, purchased item. How personal is the gift? "I gave you a Cadillac and you left me for a man who only gave you a cheap locket." "Yes, but you gave me a gift to suit your ego and his locket represents his love," came the reply in a divorce counseling session.

Sometimes codependents have trouble giving gifts of love because in their insecurity they fear they might not make the right choice. Sometimes codependents try to buy love by giving too many and too expensive gifts. Some will sacrifice things they themselves need in order to afford gifts for their loved ones. We remind such people to "love others as they love themselves." Sacrificial love, except in emergencies, is not needed and is often counterproductive.

Learning to enjoy the giving of the gift is also important. Some insecure codependent people can fret themselves into a fit worrying that their gift is not perfect enough or even worthwhile. They sometimes project their gift as an extension of themselves. Other codependents seem to give, and give, and give. Then they feel hurt because they have not received back adequate thanks or return gifts. Naturally this may be used to confirm their fear that they are not worthy and must do even more to receive some sign that they are of value to another. This, of course, is not true giving; a real gift needs no return. Giving to get is a manipulation. Giving because you enjoy the "selfish" satisfaction of choosing, making or procuring the gift, and thinking of your loved one having the gift is what a self-dependent giver does. If a strong, healthy, self-loving, self-dependent giver gets thanked for the gift, that is extra. Getting and giving the gift should be the source of the enjoyment.

At the point the gift is handed over, the strongly self-dependent person is done with it. It is completely given away, no strings attached. Many codependent people unknowingly attach strings to the gift. As one man put it, "I never really gave a gift before; I always gave in the hope that they would like me better or overlook my faults more. I gave to counterbalance what I thought were my inadequacies, and to make up for my imagined deficiencies. Therefore when giving I was always anxiously wondering if my gift would be liked, would be right, or would be enough. Now I give because I like to, and if they do not have sense enough to enjoy the gift that usually tells me something about them, not me. The minute it leaves my hand, I happily go on to the next thing. Of course, I might have chosen a poor gift and I need to consider that. Also if they want to thank me, don't get me wrong, I enjoy the hell out of their gift of thanks. But you see I am not dependent on that thanks anymore and it really feels great to realize that."

When helping couples learn how to do real, tangible, gift giving, we sometimes do several interesting training exercises. In couple's weekend workshops everyone makes their mate a homemade valentine—choosing words, colors, and materials. They go up to their mate and start to turn away, as they hand the valentine to them. They don't even have a chance to see their mate's face, thus cutting off almost all feedback potential. Then comes the hard part for the codependent mates. They must carefully look at and read the valentine they just received. They are strongly admonished never, yes never, to ask for feedback on how their mate liked the valentine they gave them. Then we ask the question, "Can you just let the giving of the gift be enough?" We also discuss the question, "Did you spend more time appreciating the valentine you got, or wondering and worrying about how well the valentine you gave was received?" Many codependent people admit they are unable to concentrate on the valentine they received, because they are obsessed with what their mate was thinking of the one they gave.

Naturally in life the giving of a gift and receiving thanks and seeing true appreciation of the gift sets up a wonderful joint experience of love. However, to do this the codependent person must first learn to give without attaching their need for reassurance. To give without real concern for getting in return, makes the giving a true gift of love. Paradoxically this later allows a person to truly appreciate thanks and to enjoy the receiver's reaction without worry.

Commonly codependents overlook, or purposely avoid, one of the very best forms of tangible gift love: that of the tangible experience. Giving the gift of an experience is often much more threatening to a highly codependent person. In one way of looking at it we give an object so that a person will have the "experience" of the gift, the experience of opening and reading the card, the experience of seeing the present for the first and perhaps repeated times, and the experience of owning the gift. The object stimulates the experiencing. Giving an "experience gift" to a person goes directly to the experiencing. Giving someone a surprise party, a vacation, a full-body massage, a ticket to a concert, these are examples of experience gifts that convey love. One of the best love gifts I ever got was a very sexy kidnapping complete with blindfold, being fed mysterious, delicious tidbits, exotic aromas and a feather massage. Wow, what a memory.

What makes the experience gift so hard for the codependent to give is that there are multiple parts that can go wrong, be imperfect, and be negatively compared with some other experience. Until a couple defeats their codependency issues, they are very likely to get into a rut and do only the things they have done before. Safety becomes much more important than the richness of widely experiencing the adventures of love. Sadly this very safety often leads to a situation where the crisis of breakdown and breakup are the only stimulation which adds misdirected adventure and variety. In fact, it is thought that many codependent couples subconsciously sabotage their dull, safe routine with crises just to get some excitement going in their lives.

Far better is the couple who will put positive variety in their life by spicing things up with tangible and experience gifts. Many codependent couples never have anyone come to their homes because they believe their house is not good enough. They will not go anywhere with others because their clothes are not good enough. They will not go out as a couple because they might bump into someone and be expected to be entertaining, or be judged, or be diverted, and excuses ad infinitum. Fear-based dependency on safety leads many couples to stagnate and deteriorate. Learning to jointly create new experience gifts of love for each other is essential. The couples that dare to help each other put new experiences in their lives, are the couples that survive and thrive.

Tangible gifts of love, like each of the other major types of love behaviors, also have effects on our health. Dr. Hans Selye, one of the most respected stress researchers, discovered that people who behaved with what he called "altruistic egoism" lived longer and healthier lives and handled their stressors far better. Altruistic egoism essentially means people give themselves a dose of good feeling (healthy self-love) by giving beneficial things and experiences to others. This is often done anonymously because the giving is what gives them their reward (1976).

Naturally receipt of a gift can also do a lot of good, especially if the gift is needed for health and well-being. A lady whose ex-husband secretly paid for her hospitalization and treatment for drug dependency, without ever being asked, gave her a wonderful gift of love. He said, "Actually, it probably did me as much good as it did her, because finally I gave without trying to get something in return."

Tangible objects and experiences of love can bring elation, help to create very special moments and memories, and provide other very important and superb feelings. Getting a gift tells me you thought of me, you went out of your way for me, you spent your energy on me, I must be special—I am loved.

CoRecovery . . . 7

What Connects Your Love With Mine?

Your have been introduced to seven of the eight major ways people show love. The eighth way of loving is a catalyst that makes the other seven ways succeed in relationships. It provides the connection and stimulates the *cycle of love.*

Receptional Loving - ***Your Love for Me Feels Wonderful.***

Codependents usually have the most trouble with receptional love. Receptional love is defined as acts and words demonstrating a positive, well-felt reception of any of the other forms of loving behavior. To show or demonstrate that you have really received and benefitted by another's act of love is, in itself, an act of love. If you hear "I love you" and really feel loved, it is far better to sincerely say something like "I feel your love for me and it feels wonderful" rather than the perfunctory "I love you, too." The reception response shows an act of love has reached you, and that is, in turn, an act of loving another.

Acknowledge that you really have been positively affected by another's attempt to show you love. It is the best response because it establishes a positive feedback loop in the interaction. Couples need to honestly show that they really received and are nourished by each other's acts of love. This return response can be done in any of the seven ways of behaving lovingly. The card that says "Thank You" is a tangible gift. The hug in response to receiving love is tactile; the smile and tones of happy words are expressional and verbal, and so on. Quite destructively our culture teaches most of us not to be good receivers. The popular response to praise is supposed to be something like a self-demeaning "it wasn't anything." Instead, I suggest a healthful, "I'm so glad you noticed; I like hearing that." In our attempt to escape egotism and self-aggrandizement we have gone too far into self-destructive and relationship-depriving abasement. If you compliment me for something I've accomplished and I say "Yes, I agree I did that quite well, and your compliment feels really good to me," my response loves us both. If instead I say "I just got lucky," or in any other way demean my accomplishment, I act to deny and cancel your act of valuing and admiration. "You did great" can be met with "You're right!" and a big smile. Many people find this type of response surprising and refreshingly honest. True egotism is going on and on about attributes or accomplishments. Receptional love replies are brief and to the point.

So many codependent people are desperately hungry for love. Unfortunately when love is sent their way, a program in their subconscious acts to block, dodge and deny the very acts conveying love. Telling an actively codependent person they are wonderful will often get a reply of "No I'm not," "If you only knew the real me, you wouldn't say so," plus a confession of shortcomings. Dodging is done by changing the subject, shifting the focus as in "Oh no, you're the one who is wonderful. I'm not much compared to you." There are a host of other elaborate thoughts and behaviors subconsciously designed to make sure the codependent does not really receive, in any deep way, the love they so greatly need and want. Loving a rigidly codependent person who uses these forms of denial is hard work.

In CoRecovery self-reprogramming work we often ask spouses to give each other compliments and praise. Their mates must only reply with words like "You're so very right" or "That's correct, I am wonderful." It is amazing how many codependent people want to reply "I can't say that." Some even feel sick because their program for denial of receiving direct love is so strong. Some play the more artful dodger and say the right words but giggle, laugh and make a parody of good healthy love reception. With coaching and practice they usually get past these impediments. They can learn to receive and accept the nourishment of the love being sent to them.

The lack of good receptional love can totally wreck a marriage. Sometimes we catch these relationships just before they are about to destruct; and sometimes we don't. As one fellow in counseling so aptly put it, "Nothing I ever did to show you love really worked. I never seemed to reach you. That's why I want a divorce. I've found other women who can really soak up love. I want to know my love does some good. I want to know it helps; that it makes a difference. When I tried to show you love it was always like trying to send it through a brick wall. You seem so impervious to me and the love I have to give. If only I could have seen my love helped you to be stronger, happier, or anything else I would have known I was important to the relationship." This relationship had nearly ended, but the couple made a surprising comeback. It only happened after this lady learned she could receive. With good reception came a growth of her self-love which, in turn, enabled her to accept love deeply and acknowledge that reception.

Some people are fond of saying that you must first love yourself before you can adequately love or be loved by another. This is an oversimplification of the truth. It's more of a simultaneous feedback loop of receiving love, loving yourself because you have received love, being able to receive more love because of that, and later being able to give love because you have both received love from others and from yourself. In this way a growing loop of love interactions fulfills my favorite dictum, "Love others as you love yourself, not after, or before, but as." Nothing demonstrates this better than good receptional love. As you act to love me, I act to receive it, and I act to show you that I received your love. This sends love to you, and if you show me that you received my expression of receiving love, we are both loving ourselves as we love each other; a wonderful, even magical set of close, intimate, good, beneficial, feelings result.

Good receptional love results in very specific physical health benefits. Dr. Glaser found that those who received love well, and thus perceived themselves to be well-loved in their mated relationships, had significantly better-functioning immune systems, a better percentage of T-Cells which help fight disease, and better ratios of lymphocytes which help suppress infection (Glaser *et al* 1984).

In CoRecovery work we do many things to help couples become good at receptional love. One of these is to have a spouse say to their mate various affirmative statements. Then the spouse, working on reception, repeatedly restates the messages. Sometimes the replies are something like "You really see me as being a kind person. And that is what I am! I am kind and you respect and admire my kindness. I really am kind and my kindness counts. My kindness is wonderful, and nothing cancels that out. I'm kind and that's a part of being the unique, wonderful me."

At first the statements sound silly or perfunctory and shallow. Often the receiver feels embarrassed and phony. With their mate helping by quietly repeating the words, "Yes, that's right. Yes you are" and giving them gentle squeezes of encouragement, they slowly begin to master reception. When people start to feel really loved, they are described as "glowing." Seeing people truly feel deeply loved is awesome. In more than one CoRecovery group I have seen every member of the group deeply touched, some with tears of shared joy. Many group members personally relate to what they witness. For the first time, in perhaps a lifetime, this recovering codependent feels loved. I have seen this emotional response from tough truck drivers, tragically hardened police detectives, emotionally indifferent scientists, accountants, engineers, pseudosophisticates, cowboys and very controlled military commanders. The power of love shown, love received, and thus love shared, never ceases to amaze me.

For couples to be good at love both must receive well. When we first therapeutically applied Swenson's findings to showing love, it did not work quite right. We noted a problem first in the area of sexuality and showing love. We realized that people have to get good at receiving love for demonstrated love to do them any good. Showing good love reception itself is an act of giving love to another. When we added this eighth element to Swenson's seven, we doubled our rate of success in sex therapy (Cookerly and McClaren 1982). Later we therapeutically applied all eight ways in the larger areas of love and codependency and we got similarly good results.

A couple may decide that the love they have for each other is not mated or marital love and consequently it is best they go different ways. However, their love bond frequently remains strong. One wife in a CoRecovery group session once read to her soon-to-be-divorced husband this tender message: "I know I will always love you and you will always love me, and we will always be showing each other love in one fashion or another. I feel quite certain of that since you know I am naturally lesbian, and I can only feel really married to another woman. I know that with sadness you are happy for me to come to a resolution of our age-old conflicts about this. You are like flesh of my flesh, and heart of my heart. You are the wonderful coparent of our children, and we will always act to love our children, each other, and our very puzzled families together. We will be like brother and sister in our love, not husband and wife. If I felt I could be heterosexual, I'd try to love you like a lover. I've tried for years to do just that, as you know. Let us go on now in our sibling love. I know I can never stop loving you, for real love must go on, as they say, 'forever.' Your love has helped me grow, helped me heal, helped me be free to love. Had I not learned to receive your love I would be dead by my own hand. Thank you so much for your life-saving and life-giving love. I love you so very, very much." Her husband did a very good job of receiving this message and with sweet, sad, feelings, they went on to be wonderful for each other in new ways. Even when couples divorce, they can find ways to do so with love if they work at it hard enough. For this, too, they must be especially good at giving and receiving love.

The Mysterious Ninth Form of Loving

Let me tell you a research finding that many scientists find hard to accept.

Dr. Randy Byrd, a cardiologist, while serving as an assistant professor of medicine at the University of California, did a well-controlled study in "distant healing." He took 393 coronary patients at San Francisco General

Hospital and had 192 of them prayed for by people around the United States who did not know and had never met them. Each patient had from five to seven people altruistically (i.e., lovingly) pray for them each day. The remaining 201 patients had no one praying for them in the network that had been set up for this experiment. The two groups had been matched with each other for severity and type of coronary difficulty and many other factors. The study went on for ten months. The prayers were for beneficial healing and quick recovery of each patient.

The results showed that the prayed for group had statistically significantly better outcomes than the control or unprayed-for group. Those prayed for had fewer medical complications and far fewer needed antibiotics. Only six of the prayed-for group suffered pulmonary edema while 18 of the unprayed-for group experienced this potentially dangerous problem. None of those prayed for needed to have tubes inserted while 12 of the unprayed-for group needed this added treatment. In all these and other ways the altruistically or lovingly prayed for group experienced an easier healing process and quicker recovery than did the unprayed-for group (Beecher 1986).

"God is love" says John in the Christian New Testament. Love, as a spiritual or divine phenomenon, is acclaimed in Judaism, Hinduism, Buddhism, Taoism and a host of other religions around the world. When a couple engages in praying for each other's health and well-being; when a couple tries to directly send each other emanations of their love; and when a couple has strong real love for one another, does something beyond our present knowledge happen that benefits them? Do those who love each other have some extrasensory love linkage that causes one to be somehow affected when the other is affected? Countless anecdotal accounts exist that tell of one mate feeling something when their distant loved one has a strong experience. Countless are the records of spontaneous recovery from serious illness when a loved one arrived on the scene, or acted in a way that conveyed love. Countless still are the people who have come back after being declared dead, stating that they came back because of a loved one.

To me it seems quite practical to help couples add a spiritual dimension to the ways they try to show each other love. Couples I have known report feeling their love much more strongly during and after various spiritual practices with each other. Most pray or meditate together. Some do these activities apart focusing on their mate with love. Some couples light candles, some chant, some ring bells, some sing hymns, some have even done liturgical dances together. Many read or recite religious or inspirational literature and sayings. Those following native American customs report amazing closeness when doing a ritual sweat. Others state that ceremonies involving food and drink have been very meaningful to the growth of their love together. A great many couples tell of times together simply looking at the stars, or a distant horizon which yielded a great loving spiritual togetherness.

One danger exists. Many codependent people are contaminated or conflicted over a destructive religious training in their background. I have heard many couples try to control each other using scripture. "A power trip is a power trip, not a love trip, Bible verse or no Bible verse," one frustrated mate responded to her Bible-thumping husband. "Religion is just fire insurance and I'm not buying yours," one man told his holier-than-thou mate. "Isn't it all just a big I'm okay, you're not okay game?" one couple asked when they were queried by a CoRecovery group member to comment on the idea of a higher power.

A lively discussion followed that helped several members clarify their spiritual understanding and apply it to their relationship. Some religious groups program people more for guilt and shame than for love and a sense of the spiritual. I recall one older couple who described themselves as spiritual agnostics. They doubted all religions, but had themselves created rituals of "spiritually connecting," which they practiced regularly.

The "how-to's" of exploring spiritual relationships are sometimes discussed in CoRecovery sessions. To explore and to experiment as a couple, not so much in religion as in spirituality, is an idea many couples find useful. Sometimes the restrictiveness of religious judgmentalism stands in the way of this, and it takes a lot of love to overcome condemnation and to replace it with forgiveness and democratic acceptance. Some people have been so turned-off by the negativism and antiloving actions of some churches that they find even terms like "spiritual" and "higher power" offensive and suspect. The antisex stances of certain religious groups especially has led to many problems in some couples' relationships. With love these problems can often be overcome.

One little example: A couple decided to marry in the church of his upbringing. Her sister and brother wanted to sing a duet as a loving gift. The song they chose was quite special to the couple. The minister asked to see the words and music. He and the church's wedding committee forbade the song because it had "start a family" in it. This was perceived as far too sexual and therefore, sinful. There was a big hubbub and everyone was taking sides. But the couple's love surmounted these difficulties. They met with everyone involved and explained that their feelings about this song were obviously "love-centered" not "sex-centered." A love-based solution resulted; they included the song, with a slight change in the words.

There are many horror stories far more severe than this little incident which have been committed in the name of religion and have been destructive to couples. Small but frequent negative incidents lead many people to be turned-off to all spiritual questioning. This can be a source of conflict among couples. There are those who are raised with severe and unhealthy religious training. There are also those who observe the problems others have with negative religious training. Both these groups may shy away from all religious or spiritual practices. Couples who can avoid being codependent on a religious perspective can find a rewarding spiritual element in their love.

One young man said, "We have a spiritual togetherness that's hard to explain. We seem to be connected to something far greater than just ourselves when we are really into our love for each other. It's entirely mysterious, but it seems very important and very helpful." His mate laughingly added, "It's strange to say this but sometimes it really seems like we can love each other with our vibes or some kind of mysterious energy."

INTEGRATION AND MASTERY

As a therapist I get to be a part of all sorts of honestly incredible love victories. That is what makes my work so gratifying. I see couples slowly, arduously and yet victoriously give up codependent behaviors and take on the ways of love. Growing love is a lifetime experience. That is the beauty of it. I am always learning new ways to demonstrate each of these eight major ways to show love. I am forever amazed at how awesome love can be. I have seen at least a thousand people grow out of despair and depression with affirmational loving. I have heard brave risks of self-disclosure love and seen healing start when this met with the acceptance and forgiveness of true tolerational love. I have observed so many couples experience the tender intimate thrill of ecstasy when expressional and verbal love met with receptional loving. I have seen the effects of loving touch save lives right in front of me. I've been told of how the right gift was incredibly precious. I have also known the all night prayer vigil when loved ones are dying. All this brings me to say, more than anything else I know of, healthy love is worth it. No set of experiences could be so great as those filled with loving.

I want to challenge you to really learn these ways of behaving with love. A single reading of these methods of demonstrating love barely introduces you to them. Now it is up to you to start putting them into your everyday life. If you do that, I think you will grow; your relationships will improve; your coupleness will expand; and you will get to experience what healthy, happy loving offers. I like to tell my patients, "Never believe what I tell you. But, never disbelieve it. Just experiment with it often enough to see if you find improvement. If you do, keep doing it. If not, junk it and do something else." However, I have never seen anyone junk love after working hard on it because the rewards are there to have. But again, don't believe me or disbelieve me. Love is more of an "action thing" than a "belief thing," so start working on your actions. Experiment with my challenge. See what happens in your life when you sincerely begin to act lovingly in each of the ways described.

I once worked with a crusty old retired colonel, who seemed to be a living example of an insurmountable obstacle to love. Near the end of our work together he said to me, "Cookerly, I thought all your love crap was just so much bullshit, so I set out to prove you wrong! Well, damn you, doing all that love crap went and made us happy. Oh, hell, I won't give you the satisfaction of saying I believe you. But I'm not about to stop doing what works."

CoRecovery . . . 8

How Do We Get the Sex Life We Both Want?

"Everything is great but our sex life. What can we do?" pleaded Debbie. Chuck, her mate, added, "Everything we try just doesn't work. We love each other, but I'm afraid we aren't sexually compatible." Most codependent couples have one kind of sex problem or another. If they do not now, they will sometime in the future. This is because in codependency, every part of a relationship is eventually affected. The good news is that the sex problems of codependency are curable.

SEX - WITH AND WITHOUT LOVE

Debbie and Chuck were skeptical and disheartened. Chuck said, "What is it going to take?" Tom, a member of their CoRecovery group answered, "It took us individual work, teamwork, knowing new things to do, and lots and lots of love." Sandra, his mate, with a broad smile added, "Self-love, self-love, and self-love. I had to learn to love all of me including my once-repressed sexy spirit, my sexy overweight body, and my wonderful, erotic mind that I didn't know I had. And I needed lots of self-love to get me through the hard times." Chuck then asked Tom what he did to improve. Tom replied, "I learned to put love into every kind of sex." "What do you mean by every kind of sex?" Debbie suspiciously inquired. Sandra with a saucy expression on her face declared, "It's moods! Sex isn't body positions, it's mind positions! At least for me it is. Mellow sex, silly sex, crude sex, romantic sex, sweet sex, primitive sex, tender sex, dirty sex, spiritual sex, dramatic sex, playful sex—with love, they're all great. I used to be so hung up, I could hardly even say the word sex." "Wow, you rattled that off so fast you must really be in touch with it now," stated Debbie enviously. Tom then said, "We had a terrible sex life until we learned how to work on it together. You have already started work by talking about it."

"That's what we can't do," Vicky, another member of the group blurted out. "We can't talk about it. We both get too ashamed or something." "I feel angry and embarrassed just listening to all of this," her husband, Wes, said with obvious aggravation. "You do seem mad," Debbie replied. "It's my defense, I guess. Whenever I feel inadequate, I start hiding behind anger," Wes admitted more softly. "Anger is what I use to get sex. Vicky, in her codependent way, gives me caretaker sex. She does just about anything to avoid my anger or to get my approval, including sex. Sometimes when I get too angry, she rescues me and protects herself by doing sex, but we never talk about it. The trouble is, it's gotten damn lonely that way. There's no real love in it—just a release."

Then Rachel, another member of the group said, "I'm starting to understand how codependency affected us. Sam and I thought sex was the one thing we were great at. We did everything: oral, anal, whips and chains, whipped cream, swinging, the works, and we liked it all. But it seemed like something was missing." Sam then spoke up. "We were searching for something, I'm not exactly sure what it was. But maybe you supplied the answer. Maybe love is missing." Rachel said, "That's right. I don't think we do love very well."

Each of these couples, in a special way, was discovering an essential truth about sex and codependency. Codependency acts to deprive a couple's sexual relationship of essential adult love experiences.

To be healthy, ongoing sexual relating requires ongoing love relating. All eight kinds of love described in the previous chapters have a contribution to make to a couple's sex life. Each helps to solve different types of sex problems. For developing healthy sexuality, each is needed in both self-love and mate-love. Knowing how to apply the behaviors of love to a couple's sexual relationship is what makes the biggest difference. That's what we discovered at our center dealing with hundreds of codependent couples with sex problems. It also was evident at the other centers and hospitals where we consulted. Every time we help a treatment facility start a CoRecovery program, learning the behaviors of love turns out to be a very important factor for overcoming sexual difficulties.

We first discovered this when we tried to cure couples' sex problems with standard sex therapy. The methods of Masters and Johnson (1970), the famous sex therapists, and Kaplan's later adaptations (1974) worked quite well. The trouble was, once the sex problem was cured, all too often the couple got divorced.

We decided to see if adding training and counseling in the eight major ways to show love would help couples stay together. By doing this we greatly accelerated the rate at which couples were getting better, helped a much larger percentage of couples overcome their sexual difficulties and greatly reduced the number of couples getting divorced (Cookerly and McClaren 1982). Then we trained other sex therapists to add the behaviors of love to their approach and discovered they got the same improved results (Cookerly and McClaren 1986). Learning to apply the behaviors of love to sexuality has produced wonderful results for many couples. Let us see how this works.

Learning the Behaviors of Love

As Debbie and Chuck explored their sex life, they told of a time when their sexual experiences together seemed to be going rather well. As time went on, the newness wore off and they just did not know how to keep their sexuality developing. They tried to enliven their sex life with sexy movies, different places and positions (the things many couples do) but nothing worked for long. It was noted in their couples CoRecovery group that whenever they talked about sex, they spoke in a serious, deadpan manner. At other times, they were rather lively. They were certainly surprised at this feedback. "Do you know who taught you to be so emotionally unexpressive about sex?" I asked. They both answered they didn't know. "So if you did know, who would it be?" I continued. "Make a wild, wrong, bad guess." Chuck, looking a little surprised, said, "For me, I think it was when my brothers and I got caught looking at a Playboy magazine. Always after that, whenever we laughed or even smiled, my father would start preaching to us about the evils of sex. I never thought of it before, but just about anytime any of us would show we were having fun, we'd get accused of thinking dirty thoughts. My dad's way of being religious was to be really down on sex. I see it now; when there's a sex problem I get somber, just like I did when Dad was around." Debbie chimed in with, "I follow your lead. When I see you so flat and dull I get that way too. When we are flat and dull about sex, we're not showing each other any love." "That's right," said Chuck. "We already know how to do better than that. Can you help us get past this?"

We then did an exercise whereby each partner looked at their mate and asked for certain tones of voice, facial expressions and postures as they talked about sex. Some silliness and embarrassment came first, but as the couples kept practicing genuine expressiveness began to occur in all but one couple. Vicky and Wes just listened, but with interest. Very powerful expressional love demonstrations, mixed with lots of sexiness, filled the room. Debbie and Chuck gave themselves a homework assignment. They would go home, get naked, and do the same thing they were doing in the CoRecovery group—talk about sex with lots of expressional loving. They would also command the antisex messages in their heads to shut up and get out of their bedroom. A week later, they reported still working on it, but making good headway. A month later they very lovingly said, "We're ready to graduate from this group. Even our sex life is great."

Vicky and Wes who, at first, could not even talk about sex, also started to improve. They demonstrated another problem so common with codependents. Extremely opposite backgrounds can lead to the same place.

Vicky and Wes could not figure out why they felt so unable to talk about sex because they thought they came from exactly opposite types of backgrounds. In Vicky's background—a little rural town, school, and home—no one ever talked about sex. In Wes's home, sex was talked about negatively every day. Vicky quickly came to understand that by never hearing sex mentioned she was thoroughly trained never to speak of it herself. Knowing this, however, only helped a little. Wes revealed that the way sex was discussed in his home and big-city neighborhood was crude and rude. Wes almost daily was made the brunt of his parents' and older sisters' jokes. They ridiculed his natural curiosity about sex and made fun of his first interest in girls. "Did you get any?" "Bet you can't get it up, shrimp" were among the mildest comments that came his way. He often avoided going to the bathroom at home because he would hear someone say, "Stop beating off and get out of there, I need to use the john." Everybody then would laugh including Wes, but his laughter wasn't real.

As he recalled all this, he shook with rage. He cussed at his parents for their assaults and for not protecting him; he denounced his sisters for their insensitivity and he cried and cried and cried. Yet, though he felt much release, he still could not readily talk about his sexual feelings.

Verbal love exercises soon changed this. He and his wife practiced tenderly including terms of endearment like "honey" and "darling" in their guided attempts to communicate about sex. Soon, their awkwardness gave way to simple, honest statements of desire and appreciation. Some standard sex therapy was added to speed their CoRecovery. Vicky said it well when she said, "Talking sex now for us is talking a very sweet form of love." Wes added, "It's amazing how close I feel when we put words of love with words of sex. I never knew people really did that." Vicky had additional work to do to overcome her caretaker sex approach. However, now that they could talk about sex, it was much easier.

Many codependent relationships are filled with sexual shame, guilt, and embarrassment, dragged along from earlier experiences like excess baggage cluttering up the couple's lifespace. Affirmational loving often helps best here. Affirmations of self-love about one's sexuality help when repeated often and with intensity. "I'm sexual and that's holy and righteous and sacred," was one woman's ardent chant. It helped her overcome the years of incest from her father, who used to whip her for her "filthy seductions" after forcing her to have sex with him. Affirmations of high worth, value, and loveability from a mate make sexual experiences a way of showing love—not simply just sex.

Material gifts can sometimes add a lot. Lovingly laughing with sexy cards, sexy underwear, vibrators and other sex toys is a way many couples learn to show their mix of sex with love. Good receptional love is needed, of course. "We're enshrining the vibrator he got me," joked one woman. "When he learned to hold it and me at the same time, my fear of abandonment got replaced with the neatest sense of closeness," she explained.

Tactile loving is a crucial need among many couples suffering from codependency connected sex problems. Martha told a story that carried a message. "We both kept having affairs," she confessed. "I'd catch Nate in bed with some airhead and just have to get even. So I'd end up in bed with one bozo or another. We made sure it was never anybody to worry about, except for disease. Diseases worried me a lot. I made sure he knew it; and then we'd have a fight. I mean, a real fight. I'd start hitting him and get slapped around. Then we'd cry a lot, make up, forgive each other, and promise never to do it again. Then we'd make violent love. I don't know which hurt more, the fights or the sex. I suppose it had to do with the dysfunctional homes we grew up in. Both of us never got hugged or held, just slapped around a lot, so what could you expect? A whipping meant somebody cared. Then we came here and learned about loving touch. God, what an incredible difference that's made. Now we lay around for hours lightly caressing and filling up on how special and precious we are to each other. It's heaven."

Dealing with Severe Sexual Problems and Codependency

Self-disclosure loving has to be matched with tolerational loving to help many couples get past their sex problems. This is especially true for severe sexual problems involving codependency. A lot of codependency is linked to backgrounds in which there was substance abuse. The children of drug users, alcoholics and even prescription addicts often have been overtly or covertly abused sexually. With tragic regularity sex problems in adulthood are the result of such abuse. The behavioral addictions of parents also can lead to sexual abuse. A workaholic spouse is never home. Their mates turn to a son or daughter to fill their unmet adult needs and an emotional incest develops that warps the child. The wife or husband of a gambling addict may behave much the same seeking support from an available child. A parent addicted to religiosity may corrupt a child's natural healthy sexuality to the extent that feelings of sex and guilt seem inseparable. Extremely repressed sexuality or rebellious and compulsive acting out of every sexual impulse can be the result.

Frequently sexual abuse is repressed beyond the ability of conscious memory to recall it. As a couple's recovery progresses, it is common for their repressed memories to surface. Often before these memories emerge, the couple's sexual relationship may go through mysterious changes. Hypersexuality, antisexuality, or blah sexuality may appear. Conflict is common with each change. The very growth of loving in the relationship creates a sense of safety. This causes the subconscious to release the memories of abuse. At these times tolerational loving must match self-disclosure. Showing you my ugly, unhealed emotional wounds is a great risk of intimate sharing. You may reject me for having these wounded parts. Can you love me even though I have damaged and dysfunctional parts? If you can, I may more readily heal. If you can't, our relationship may be damaged.

Making the issue even harder is the fact that feelings about an event often emerge before memories of the event itself surface. Sharon, who was a rather quiet, shy, woman told her CoRecovery group that she had suddenly starting having episodes of wanting to scream and even hit her mate, Terry, for no apparent reason. This was even more baffling because recently, Terry had become both more loving and happier. Sharon was able to see that Terry's loving had helped her have a new sense of safety in the relationship.

I asked her when these episodes had begun. It was after she and Terry had been too tired to make love but they had masturbated beside each other finding that felt intimate together and not as exhausting as their usual love making. After a nap, Sharon woke up feeling hateful.

I asked what she had been taught about masturbation as a child. She looked afraid and began to weep, although she still could not say why. Then suddenly, she trembled and remembered a period of her childhood that had always been blank. Starting at the age of 11, her mother had repeatedly beaten her for masturbating. Once she had come home from school smiling and her mother beat her saying that smile meant she had masturbated. That was when her shy, quiet, wallflower ways began. As she told of these beatings, great rage and sorrow poured out.

After a long hard session of working through her feelings she first asked Terry, and then the whole group, to hold and rock her. As that happened tears of relief and a general relaxation occurred. She later reported that since she and Terry shared that experience in the group, she felt lighter and more free. She now understood that her past programming was to act out the role of her mother and that's why she wanted to hit and scream at Terry after masturbating. Sharon and Terry's experience is fairly typical, one in which one partner has experienced severe abuse connected to sexuality. First, the feelings emerge irrationally. If these are lovingly dealt with, then the actual memories come forward and can be resolved.

Many mates do not handle things as well as Terry did. Terry had been learning about tolerational loving and self-love. Without these, Terry might have gotten mad, hurt, felt blamed or had a host of other typical negative reactions. Terry did have one common reaction usual to mates of the abused; he got very mad at Sharon's parents, until he saw that Sharon felt abandoned by his focusing on them instead of on her. Vengeance against the perpetrator provides no love for the victim. Vengeance might help the mate of the abused feel better, but it usually helps the victim feel worse, and that continues their victimization. If they are suffering from codependency, handling the vengeful mate means an additional burden. Love shown to the victim/spouse is what really helps.

After incest and child molestation there can be an additional problem. "If I tell Les I was forced to have sex with my parents, Les will think I'm damaged goods," Marilyn said in a private session after finally admitting memories of incest into her awareness. "Won't you always be afraid of Les finding out and be a little distant if you don't tell him?" I asked. "Yes, I guess we'll never be as close as I'd like because of that, but I don't want to risk losing him," Marilyn said. Marilyn and I discussed various ways she might more safely work past this problem. Later in their CoRecovery group, Marilyn was able to ask Les to be full of tolerant love so she could tell him the most intimate truths about her past. When she revealed the incest Les was mad. Then one of the other husbands said, "You are doing the same thing I did. You are coming from ownership, not from love. It sounds to me like you feel like you possess a used object and you thought you had a new one. Are you going to love her or own her? I found I couldn't do both, so I picked love. I hope you have sense enough to do the same. If you don't, she deserves someone better." Les had to do some work on his self-love. Then he had to achieve a deeper understanding of tolerational love. He did both of these beautifully, and in doing so he and Marilyn grew to a remarkable closeness.

With enough training and counseling in how to love their way through problems, lots of couples can find that their joint victories bring a great sense of solid closeness. "We've loved each other through so much and that's brought us so close. I'd never want anyone else no matter how attractive she was. It would be like starting over in kindergarten when I'm already in graduate school," said one happy CoRecovering spouse.

How Our Culture Sexually Abuses Us

In a sense, aspects of our culture are like a bad marriage that sexually abuses its children. One part of our society acts like a compulsive sex addict, constantly obsessed with sex. Every waking hour of a sex addict's life can involve doing something about sex. This activity may be connected to deception, violence, drugs, and lots of other destructive things. But love is noticeably absent. Another part of our culture is like a compulsive sex phobic who, without love, attempts to suppress and condemn sexuality in all but the narrowest of ways. The two form a marriage in which we grow up, bombarded by these two contradictory sides. They vie for our allegiance like two parents wanting the children to be on their side against the other parent. Both are equally sexually abusive because neither comes with sufficient love. The result is sexually confused and conflicted children who grow up to pass on the same system to their offspring.

Few people grow up in our culture without sexual conflicts. Fewer still are the love relationships that are free from sexual conflict. With codependency the sexual problems inflicted upon us by our sexually discordant culture are magnified. The codependent tendencies to be inappropriately controlling, caretaking, rescuing, self-sacrificing, self-degrading and all the rest enter into the couple's sexual relationship. Too much loveless sex or too little sexual love is the usual result.

Healthy sexual self-love frequently has to be a part of the cure. Our culture is negative about that; and most codependents have internalized the negativity. Gus put it well in working with his wife, Holly. "When we do wild, passionate sex, I really feel like a man. Afterwards, I beat up on myself for acting like an animal and I feel ashamed. When we do tender, sweet sex I feel close and in love, but afterwards I hear messages in my head telling me I'm a wimp, I could be homosexual, and then I feel real inadequate." Holly said, "My feelings aren't that different from yours. The wilder it gets, the more I love it. Then the next day, I'm fighting messages in my head that say I'm a slut and a whore, and I get real down on myself. When it's tender, I feel better. Then I get to thinking I'm not enough for you, Gus, and I feel inadequate." To help themselves, Gus and Holly invented a little ritual. They go into their bedroom and tell the whole culture to "get stuffed." They are going to do sex anyway they please. Then they make love anyway they want to. If either of them feels bad afterwards, they go through their little ritual again. This "telling off" the culture that programmed them for sexual failure was a major step in their building a healthy, loving sex life together.

Many codependent's sex problems have long remained needlessly uncured. Our society's shame-training about sex is at the root of this problem. Nan had never climaxed; she and Murray went for help. Nan was told learning to masturbate and be masturbated by her mate was a usual part of the cure. She refused to continue sex therapy because she had been taught that masturbation was a sin. Not long after, Murray began having affairs, which he made sure Nan learned about. All the usual agonies of a codependent relationship ensued. In desperation, Murray and Nan entered CoRecovery counseling. Soon they were telling their story in couple's group. Nan was shocked to hear that every man and almost every woman in the group had first climaxed by masturbation. Most of the women stated they thought they never would have climaxed without first learning to masturbate. Nan reentered sex therapy with Murray and fourteen weeks later, had her first orgasm. It had been eight years since her first attempt at sex therapy. Eight years of needless marital misery related to sexual difficulties. During a group session, Nan and Murray raged against all the societal influences that had blocked their sexual development. They lovingly embraced. Both said it was like a wall between them had finally come down.

As Murray and Nan continued to reprogram themselves about sexuality they discovered an interesting surprise. Nan's parents were not the primary people who had programmed her against masturbation. Her religious training, the small private school she attended, and a particularly sex-phobic aunt had been the more significant influences. Nan now saw these influences as subtle sexual abuse disguised in the name of morality and religion. Finding a new and healthier church became part of this couple's cure. Sending their children to a school where sex education was not training in antisexuality was also important. Training their children in natural and healthy concepts about sexuality, including masturbation, was something Nan and Murray integrated into their parenting.

Pia Mellody, one of the foremost authorities on codependency in individuals, says, "Masturbation is part of normal development. It's how we keep our brain, which is our master sex gland, connected to our genitals which is one of the main places we experience sexual stimulation. Masturbation helps us become sexually functional adults. It's completely inappropriate to tell a child that masturbating is abnormal" (1989,158).

Couples who work to defeat their codependency often have to reevaluate how their upbringing is still effecting their sexuality. Many who do this focus only on the experiences they received in their family-of-origin. Societal and cultural effects are given too little attention. Frequently, it is not until we learn that other cultures are really different from ours that we see there is more than one way to do things. The commonness of full nudity of both sexes on Scandinavian T.V., people urinating in public in central European countries, groups of children blithely passing neighborhood sex shops with explicit pictures in the windows in Germanic countries, naked people of all ages on the nude beaches of the Aegean Sea, people making love in the ads of European magazines have all been known to shock Americans abroad; yet they are commonplace in much of the Western world. Some Americans are even more astonished to meet the several wives of an Islamic husband or see the public parade of phalluses in Japan. When viewed from cross-cultural perspectives, our society's training about sex becomes quite questionable. Recently multiculturalism has been proposed as one of the most significant forces in the field of counseling (Pedersen 1991). Counseling with a multicultural emphasis is helping codependent couples. They find that discovering what is healthy for them takes looking both into and beyond the ways they were brought up.

Sexual Abuse in Our Families-of-Origin

The most severe sexual problems codependent couples face often involve overt sexual abuse in their childhood. An alcoholic parent or, more recently, parents using some other substance such as cocaine, so called "designer" drugs, heroin, and the like are the perpetrators. Judgment and impulse control are eventually reduced by almost all forms of chemical addiction. Sexual abuse frequently follows. Secrecy training accompanies this. "Do not tell anyone or I will kill you" is what addicted perpetrators often tell their victimized children. This fear causes the suppression of these memories in the abused child. Years later, as the victim attempts to enter adult relationships, a sexual problem surfaces. Severe codependency is commonly part of this picture. Individual and couples therapy is usually required. Individual therapy by itself, may help the victim, but not the couple.

The added trauma of losing a spouse in divorce because of childhood sexual abuse compounds the abuse. When both partners spend enough time together in couples or group CoRecovery sessions, the divorce potential can be greatly reduced. When the mate and the adult survivor learn as a team to be skillful at love, a powerful weapon for recovery is activated. Without this skillful teamwork in giving and receiving love, the issues of sexual abuse wreak havoc in the relationship. Painful breakups are the result. Many of these can be avoided with CoRecovery work. Even when there is an end to a relationship, joint counseling has the best record for producing the least traumatic divorces (Cookerly 1976).

Psychosexual Abuse. Ted grew up in a family that sexually abused him mentally although he did not know it. When he married Stella he began to make jokes about her body. Ted laughed at Stella's way of being sexy, and told her she looked incredibly stupid when she reached orgasm. Ted's climaxes were rather restrained events. Soon, Stella's climaxes looked and sounded just like Ted's. Stella's were faked. She, in typical codependent fashion, kept her growing unhappiness secret, and always tried to please him. Her only real sexuality occurred alone with self-stimulation. She sometimes cried after her lonely climaxes. Her husband's sexual ridicule grew increasingly rude and offensive. Otherwise, Ted was fairly loving and considerate. Then one day, it was all too much for Stella. All the put-downs she had endured erupted in an angry, mocking, ridiculing attack. She laughed at the size of Ted's penis and told him his love making was the worst she had ever known, and that she had known plenty. Ted angrily counterattacked. In doing so the cause of his ridiculing became apparent, although he did not know it at the time. His counterattack was filled with statements like "You're just like my mother."

A few months after this fight, both entered counseling. Ted had not been able to get an erection since that argument. When they told about the fight, I asked Ted what he meant when he said "You're just like my mother." It all came out. Ted's mother and, in fact, his whole family constantly shamed and ridiculed each other with sexually oriented comments. As a young boy, his small penis was the brunt of many jokes. Ted saw that in marriage he had become a copy of his mother, giving the very abuse he had hated. Stella saw that she also copied what she had done in childhood. She took his verbal attacks and acted nice because it was the only safe thing to do. In her childhood, back talk was severely punished, as was any mention of sex. Sex was something she never heard around her home, so she never seriously talked about it with Ted until that fight. Once they both saw their joint system of giving and taking sexual abuse statements, they quickly changed. With love-based sex therapy they worked to develop a healthier sexuality together.

The mental form of sexual abuse can be overt or covert. Sexually charged emotional interactions between children and parents can disturb years later the psychosexual interactions of a couple. "I don't know why I feel so uncomfortable talking to my wife about sex" suggests a hidden cause in childhood. "My parents both were so seductive to me," said one woman. "Both treated me as an adult about sex when I was only six or seven," she remembered. "They would tell me about how much they made love and what they had done the night before. I just froze and hated it every time." Later, her husband's efforts to talk out their sex differences met with this same frozen reaction until counseling alleviated the problem.

Tanya said, "I was Daddy's little woman after mother left. I enjoyed the role. I felt special and I got all Daddy's attention, even his sexual attention. He never touched me sexually, but sex got to be all we ever talked about. I was only twelve when I compulsively started talking about sex to boys. Soon I was known as the school tramp. I really thought sex was the only topic I could talk about to males."

"When we were dating, I almost lost my husband, Ray, over this. Ray told me he wanted to talk to me about other things besides sex and I didn't believe him. It took me forever to find out Ray was in love with all of me and not only my sexual side. I just thought he was like Daddy and all the other guys. Once Ray got mad at me for turning every conversation into one about sex. That confused me, but I liked it. Slowly I learned to talk about everything under the sun," Tanya said.

The sexual abuse that is primarily psychological can come in many forms. Lana described hers this way. "Over and over, they told me I was a sinner. Over and over, they told me sex was sinful. Over and over, they told me they knew I had sinful ways on my mind. When I started thinking about boys, I decided they were right and I was lost. Since I was lost I concluded 'What difference does it make?' I lived up to what they had told me I was. I screwed every boy I could, and started in on girls. Finally, I met Kurt and got some real love. We had a lot of problems until I learned to love myself like he loved me. Now I don't think of myself as a sinner but as someone who has love to give and love to get. That's helped a lot."

Psychosexual abuse contaminates many couples. Decontaminating a relationship often takes counseling or therapy. A word of caution is necessary here. I am sorry to say that there are counselors who psychosexually abuse their clients, though they do not mean to. If a counselor or therapist disparages either gender, is homophobic, insists you are a victim of sexual abuse even though you are not, or sees sex in everything you say, suspect something is wrong with the counselor. Counselors and therapists who have resolved their personal sexual issues provide a balanced input. Sexual factors will be only part of their focus even if sex therapy is their specialty.

COMMON SEXUAL CONCERNS OF CODEPENDENCY

Sexual Interest Imbalances

Codependents have a high frequency of certain sexual difficulties. Imbalanced interest in sexuality is something that eventually distresses most couples who are debilitated with codependency. In many instances, as one spouse's interest in sex increases the other's declines. Sometimes both increase but are divergent. For example, one wants lighter or more playful sex while their mate desires romantically rich and emotionally meaningful lovemaking. Sometimes one person's sexuality remains about the same while their mate's changes. With each type of imbalance, many of the couple's interactions can turn negative. Codependent caretaking and controlling problems emerge. Self-love can plummet. Growing frustration leads to boundary invasions. The expression of emotions becomes extreme. In short, everything can get worse. Some codependent couples can isolate their sex problems and the rest of their relationship may not suffer severely. However, that is not common.

This problem of imbalanced interest in sexuality repeatedly arises when one mate is working to overcome codependency problems and the other spouse is not, or when one partner refuses to talk about the emerging sexual problem, read about it, or otherwise participate in a solution. These sexual imbalances in a couple can happen because one partner refuses to enter counseling with their mate. It also can occur when a counselor or treatment center treats only one spouse and virtually ignores the mate. When the couple is treated as a team, in joint counseling, the problems of imbalanced sexual interests are much more manageable. The partners learn to experiment with each other's wishes. Both partners then usually integrate their differing interests and jointly become more sexual. At first this can be a painful process because each problem is made glaringly clear. Joint counseling sessions are usually alternated with individual sessions in more severe cases. When a person is suffering from some other problem, such as an addiction or breakdown, a more individual focus may start the process. However, I usually like to include the mate in the healing process quite quickly. I also like to start the couple working together as a team early in the process of recovery if possible.

Well-communicated love is usually at the core of curing imbalanced sexual interest. Commonly one, or both, spouses need more love demonstrated along with an interest in sex. "I know you like my body, but do you love me?" they ask. "Do you want me just for sex or do you want me for love?" is another way it is sometimes expressed.

A deficiency of self-love may be part of a difference in sexual interests; "When I like my own body more, I will be okay doing sex with you." Common are statements like, "I'm ashamed of myself sexually, so it's hard for me to want to make love with you." Even more common are people who hide their feelings of sexual inadequacy with feigned disinterest or blame.

Whenever the love problems get cured, the sex problems get easier to address. "Now that I feel really loved, I want to do sex with you more," becomes the new type of statement heard in CoRecovery. Love alone does not solve all the problems. A couple will still need to experiment with each other's desires and integrate their sexual differences. Well-communicated love, however, does make this much easier.

Affairs - Causes and Cures

Sex outside the relationship is often a heavy concern among couples afflicted with codependency. Turning away from a mate and turning toward another when feeling unloved often occurs. Some mates try to break a dependency on their spouse by having an affair. Codependent jealousy and rebellion can lead to retaliatory, extramarital sex. Generally speaking, codependency can make sex outside the relationship more likely. This is often vaguely understood by one partner or the other. Extra controlling behaviors often result; and they usually backfire.

It is important to see that illicit sex outside of the relationship results from occurrences inside the relationship. It is inappropriate to fault either partner alone. It is the relationship system that is at fault, if fault must be found. Dr. Marilyn Mason, a well-recognized therapist in codependency work put it well when she said, "Neither partner realizes at the time that he/she is in collusion with the other; extramarital sex is always at least a two-person affair. One partner does not walk out the door unless the other is knowingly or unknowingly holding it at least partially open."(1988,67)

Shame, remorse, resentfulness, blame and guilt are added to the couple's problem when affairs begin to surface. Sometimes people get caught on purpose to end the guilt or bring the intolerable situation to a head. Occasionally, that helps. Sometimes it takes a very dramatic event for some couples to make up and work on their relationship. "I absolutely hate to say it," Jack said, "but Karla's affair is what saved us. I never would have changed my ways until I saw I really could lose her." This is a dangerous way to go. Breakdowns, suicides, and murder are all too common when affairs happen; sexually transmitted disease is also a possibility. Deciding to jointly work on improving love and sex is much safer. Once an affair has started or become serious, seeking a good couples counselor skilled in working with romantic triangles is advised. Some marital and family therapists do not work with people having an affair and others do, so it is wise to ask about this ahead of time.

Sexual Dysfunctions and CoRecovery

Codependency worsens and magnifies sexual dysfunctions. Both men and woman can fail to have orgasms. Codependent people are especially prone to becoming anxious about this failure. With enough anxiety, sexual physiology malfunctions. With enough anxiety men can fail to have an erection. Women may fail to lubricate and intercourse becomes abrasive and painful. Anxiety in a couple's sex life may cause premature ejaculation. Thus a self-fulfilling prophecy is born.

Awkward performance, a desire just "to get it all over with," or not do it at all are dysfunctions that can stem from insecurity and anxiety in a couple's sexual interactions. Whatever the sexual problem, professional help is available and usually works. (For referral to Certified Sex Therapists and Sex Counselors see the Resource Guide at the back of this book.) Many codependent couples must face sexual dysfunctions that have their roots in sexual abuse and trauma. The more love the couple knows how to give and receive, the quicker couples usually can overcome these traumatic influences. I remember Martha who suffered from vaginismus and said, "When Lester got good at being gentle, I started remembering how my sisters forced things in me that hurt. It wasn't until then that I loosened up and let him in. I knew he wasn't going to hurt me. He likes being gentle with me." As couples apply the behaviors of love, even the most difficult of sexual dysfunctions can be ameliorated.

A Couple's Approach to the Problems of Sex Addiction

Some codependents face problems with obsessive and compulsive sexual behaviors. Sex can turn into an addiction interfering with love, recreation and even work. Sally said, "I kept getting fired for having sex on the job. I lost two good jobs and one bad one, before I figured out I had a problem. Ray, my husband, was about to leave me over it and my kids were real upset. The worse things got at home, the more I had to have sex with someone at work or someplace. Then I would get fired and home would get worse. It was a horrible cycle. Self-help groups, Twelve Step programs, therapy and a couple's CoRecovery program helped Sally and Ray interrupt their destructive cycle and move on to healthy behaviors.

This destructive cycle is common to many couples troubled by sex addiction issues. If both partners are sexually addicted the destructive cycle is accelerated. In this case both sex addicted partners may support each other's denial that there is a problem until something truly drastic occurs. Some couples don't realize something is wrong until one or both have been arrested, violently attacked, or become diseased through their compulsive sexual behaviors.

To begin the process of recovery a couple must honestly start accessing the sexual situation. If one or both are constantly pursuing sexual pleasure to the exclusion of most other healthful enjoyments, a problem probably exists. If sex is repeatedly interfering with the duties of responsible living, a problem probably exists. If sexual activity repeatedly means other aspects of healthful living are damaged, a problem probably exists. If any of these are occurring, get professional help.

In my experience, couples working as a team in counseling against sexual additions accomplish far more than do individuals working separately in treatment. So often in the background of sex addiction is a confusion between love and sex. I have found that couples trained in the eight major ways humans show love can more rapidly and thoroughly sort through this confusion.

As couples share their work on sex addiction both tolerational and self-disclosure loving are especially important. With these the root causes of the problem usually come to light and strategies for dealing with them can be planned. Delving into and understanding the root causes of sex addiction can be a rough time for a couple. Sometimes tolerational love is the only thing that gets them through this period.

Geraldine and Henry were referred after she had been diagnosed as having a life-threatening disease. Shortly after the diagnosis, Geraldine began compulsive sexual behaviors including incessant masturbation, seductions of other men and constantly wanting sex with Henry. Henry was beside himself with anger, anxiety, and massive confusion. With counseling that included a crash course in tolerational loving Henry was less hostile. In working with a less angry, less codependent, and more effectively supportive Henry, Geraldine confessed she had had similar problems before marriage. Her marriage seemed to have provided her with sufficient love and security, consequently a remission of her problem had occurred. We looked into Geraldine's background and before long found the origin of her difficulties. "My aunt was the only happy person in my miserable childhood," Geraldine said. "I used to peek into her bedroom from the porch when I heard her giggling at night. Many times I'd seen her and one of her boyfriends really enjoying themselves sexually. When I did this I was fascinated, entertained, and totally distracted from my problems. Later when I was sad, troubled, or anxious I'd turn to sex and pretend to be my aunt. Sex became the one sure way to feel good about my life. It was my medicine for every trouble," Geraldine related. I suggested when Geraldine found out how sick she was she might have automatically regressed to taking care of herself with sex as she had in the past. Geraldine said she felt that really was true. Hearing all of this, compassion replaced confusion in Henry's mind. With new understanding, Henry and Geraldine were able to work out new strategies to fight the sex addiction. Love interactions soon replaced Geraldine's compulsive sex behaviors. They proved to be much more effective in providing reassurance, good feelings and distraction from her illness.

It is important to know that some authorities believe certain cases of sex addiction may be caused by hormonal or hypothalamic disorders. Even under these circumstances couples can work as a loving team to counter the symptoms of sex addiction.

Incest, Molestation and Sexual Violence

Codependents sometimes come from backgrounds where there has been incest, sexual violence or sexual molestation. With great anguish they sometimes discover that they have impulses to perpetuate these acts on others. How we were treated can subconsciously program us in how to treat others, even when we vow to be different.

Brenda was mortified as she told of wanting her husband to have sex with their daughter. She fought the fantasy until one night when they both got drunk and tried to act it out. The next morning they called for help. In therapy she remembered her drug-addicted parents repeatedly taking her to their bed when she was a child.

Sometimes a couple faces the reoccurrence of victim desires. As children, Ginger and her brother, George, were both made to strip naked and were tied to a chair while their parents severely whipped them. Ginger and her husband, Harley, came for help telling of how Ginger wanted to be sexually harmed. Sometimes her fantasy desire included watching another man receiving the same punishment. It did not take long to uncover how she had been conditioned to associate nudity and sexuality with the punishments of her youth. Harley was instrumental in helping Ginger to recondition her sexual responses. Sex became associated with love instead of punishment and harm. As she recovered, she contacted her brother. He admitted having the same sort of problem and was greatly relieved to discover help was available.

In these severe cases, self-disclosure love and tolerational love are very important. When there has been incest, a whole new approach to tactile love is necessary. "I hate to be touched before and after making love," Warren reported. His wife, Vivian, loved to caress and be caressed, especially before and after making love. Warren had a childhood history of incest involving painful anal penetrations. It had always started and ended with genital caresses. Warren and Vivian understood their problem, but they did not know what to do about it. As part of their therapy our Center's Registered Massage Therapist taught them to touch each other using a progressive series of nonsexual massage techniques. It took a number of sessions before Warren could relax and enjoyably receive the pleasing touches of his mate. Warren and Vivian tried both the massages and cuddling at home for short, and then longer, periods. It took time and some other psychotherapy, but it worked. Today, Warren is known as a real toucher and Vivian says she gets stroked and cuddled all the time. A host of other sexually problematic couples have benefitted from similar retraining for loving touch.

Lesbian, Homosexual, Bisexual, and Homophobic Concerns

For a long time scientific evidence has been slowly accumulating concerning the causes of heterosexuality, homosexuality and related states. Increasingly, this evidence indicates that basic sexuality is a natural physical phenomenon. Heterosexuality, male and female homosexuality, and bisexuality occur in most species of mammals and birds studied by animal comparative psychologists, zoologists, livestock agriculturalists, and other biologically-grounded scientists. In nature dogs, cats, cows, horses, pigs, pigeons, and others exhibit all forms of sexual orientation. In the laboratory certain experiments produce increased homosexual and bisexual behaviors. Pregnant laboratory rats can be both physically and psychologically treated in such a way as to influence how many of their offspring are homosexual (Russell 1988). Recently, research in the brain's physiological structure has yielded a startling discovery. Dr. Simon LeVay of the prestigious Salk Institute found a cluster of cells that was consistently larger in heterosexual men than in homosexual men. Using microscopic examinations focusing on the anterior hypothalamus, Dr. LeVay discovered this cell cluster difference in an area known as the interstitial nuclei. This cluster is called INAH for short. Previous animal studies have identified the INAH as one of the principal roots of sexual behavior (1991).

For decades psychoanalysts, psychiatrists, and clinical psychologists have searched diligently for a psychological cause of homosexuality. Many theories have been formulated and none has ever held up under the scrutiny of replicated empirical research (Thomas 1983). Comparative psychologists, neuroanatomists and behavioral physiologists are doing much better. This does not mean that all homosexuality is definitely caused by biology alone. Humans are much more complicated than that. It does, however, strongly suggest that all forms of basic sexuality have naturally occurring biological components.

These scientific findings have many ramifications in codependency. First of all, if you know you are currently feeling quite heterosexual, you do not have to worry about being latently homosexual or, in other words, suddenly changing. Likewise, if you experience yourself as strongly homosexual or lesbian, you are not likely to suddenly become a raving heterosexual no matter what anyone does to you. If you are in a homosexual mated relationship suffering from codependency problems, there is help available. Dr. Marion Mason states "Gay-Lesbian relationships are now receiving the respect they long needed in many treatment centers.... Unless gays and lesbians are allowed to talk openly about their sexual preference they will continue to confront the same issues they had prior to treatment or involvement in AA [and other Twelve Step programs]. If human dignity is the focus of recovery—as indeed it should be—then it is only natural that all nonexploitive loving relationships be respected" (1988, 68-69).

In my experience CoRecovery counseling for male and female homosexual couples seems to work just like it does for heterosexual couples. The issues, the approaches and the solutions are much the same.

Heterosexuals married to homosexuals present different issues. One lesbian wife of a heterosexual man put it this way, "I've discovered I deeply love you, but mine is the love of a sister for a brother. Can you love me as my brother? Will you?" With work they grieved the loss of their marriage but reformed their relationship and remained close and dear to each other. Others with varying degrees of agony and acceptance have achieved healthy outcomes in this difficult situation.

Bisexuality brings another set of difficulties, also usually solvable. Unusual solutions have to be carefully custom-tailored. Arno Karlen did a twenty-year study of three-person mated relationships. In his book, *Threesomes*, he reported the existence of long-lasting, happy three-person relationships (1988). Dr. Byron Brook in his book, *Design Your Love Life,* reported similar situations (1989). Some codependent couples are attracted to such ideas but, in my experience, they are not generally able to make these unions work. Some manage brief liaisons with a third party without damage; others join swingers' clubs but become disenchanted. Most codependent couples experimenting with third parties get into a mess. Often underlying these experiments is the hope that their efforts will cure the codependent problem. Generally, the couple's relationship has to get really good before anything unusual is attempted. By then the unusual may lose its appeal.

Karla, who had had problems in this area, said, "Bisexual fantasies are all John and I need now, where before we thought we had to carry them out. Fantasies are so safe and uncomplicated, and they always work out perfectly." In CoRecovery groups it is not unusual for a fair portion of the couples to admit having bisexual ideas, urges or dreams. Finding out that this is not so unusual often helps couples relax about their bisexual fantasies. With the reduction of anxiety couples who were bisexually obsessional report that their bisexual fixation dissipates. Then a broader range of fantasies may enhance their sex life.

Many people suffering from codependency seem to think bisexual notions mean they may be latently homosexual. Most homosexuals do not fear being latent heterosexuals, but they can fear their homosexual mate is. These fears tend to be unfounded. People who experience themselves as heterosexual or homosexual may be bisexual or become bisexual. They seldom, however, switch all the way over to the other orientation exclusively. With love, and lots of careful work, couples in CoRecovery usually find ways to cope with these sexual variations and are glad to go on to other issues.

Homophobic problems can cause a most difficult complication for codependent couples. Obsessive and compulsive concern about other people's homosexuality, feelings of anger, and the desire to do violence to homosexuals marks homophobia. Out of their codependency some spouses acquiesce to their homophobic mate's violent opinions. This becomes then a hate-based or hate-contaminated relationship. Behind the hate are unaddressed fears. Sometimes the homophobic person was homosexually molested in childhood and has repressed the memory.

Lisa first complained that Mack got angry every time she wore pants. She later revealed Mack would never let her get on top during sex. In her previous marriage that was her favorite sexual position. It took a long time for Mack to decide to come to counseling. He was a small man but a supermacho type. Lisa could not have looked or acted more feminine. Mack's talk contained a lot of derogatory remarks about homosexuals. In a later couples session, Lisa mentioned that she sometimes masturbated while thinking about other females, but this wasn't a problem for her.

Mack went white. With some gentle therapeutic intervention, and Lisa's appropriate loving support, Mack relaxed enough to say he was remembering something he had long tried to forget. When he was a young boy, he had been sexually molested by older males. Ever after he had worked to develop an extremely masculine image, thinking that this would mean he could never be mistaken for a homosexual. His hate of homosexuality hid his secret fear that such a thing could happen to him again. His hate restricted his sexuality with Lisa. She was secretly very afraid of him because of his violent outbursts about sex and this caused her to be sexually guarded. Mack was not dumb. He saw that he was letting his past molestation rob him of good life experiences. He set out to overcome this, Lisa working right beside him. Mack is still macho and Lisa feminine, but hate and fear do not infect their life as it used to.

Do We Need Special Help?

Couples can do a lot by themselves. They can learn and work together to grow better sex lives. They can overcome sexual problems with love and learning. If this is not enough, couples can join support groups that deal with sexual issues and can go to sex education classes, workshops and retreats. A lot of codependents go to CoDa. Those with addictions and related issues can go to AA, NA, Al-Anon, other Twelve Step Groups, and other addiction recovery groups. All this can help, but may not be the best thing to do. Gerald Shulman, writing about sexuality and recovery says, "'Going to more meetings' is not a solution to sexual problems. 'Therapy' may be very threatening to many people in self-help groups. If the AA or Al-Anon member . . . believes that his program is the answer to all of his problems, then going into therapy may be perceived as a betrayal of AA or the indication that AA is not working. Obviously this is not the case. If an alcoholic or significant other has an attack of appendicitis, going to more meetings is not going to help" (1988,79).

CoRecovery counseling and couples group counseling work the same way. If the sexual problems are not being fixed, the addition of specialized sex therapy may be necessary.

SPIRITUAL SEXUALITY AND SEXUAL SPIRITUALITY

Four kids were talking about their bodies. The first kid said, "God made everything above the belly button and Satan made everything below." The second kid said, "If you are a girl, Satan made everything below the neck and that is why you have to keep it covered up." The third kid said, "If you are a boy, the Devil made your head where you think dirty, nasty thoughts." The fourth child said, "I was taught God made all of me and saw that it was good." Which child represents the way you were brought up? Which kid has the best chance of having a healthy sex life and what might happen to the others?

Most codependent people raised in the Judeo-Christian world have Dark Ages sex training in their subconscious. Some of these messages are: "Good" is sexless. "Evil" is sexy. God is antisex. Satan is prosex. That which is spiritual is pure and that which is pure is nonsexual. That which is secular is corrupt and that which is corrupt is saturated with sex. This kind of archaic training puts sexuality and spirituality at odds with each other.

The nonintegration of sexuality and spirituality presents a problem for the population in general and codependents in particular. For the many codependents who have been raised in religiously conservative, antisexual homes and communities the problem can be pronounced. This type of religion seems to produce more than its share of people who suffer in codependent relationships. Addiction to religiosity is often an added complication.

I have worked, taught and done research all over America and Western Europe. Everywhere there are religious movements that promote health, love, and well-being. Everywhere there are also religious groups that promote shame, guilt, dependency and psychological illness. I like to say that our Center is located in the buckle of the Bible Belt; the Dallas/Fort Worth area is where the Mid-Western prairie hooks up with the forested South. Both come with a lot of interesting religious traditions. Besides these all the transplanted easterners, northerners, and Hispanics add their religious customs, making it even more interesting. Now our Buddhist, Islamic, and Hindu populations are growing rapidly. This religious mix has challenged our CoRecovery program to help a lot of religiously varied couples to grow a compatible spiritual understanding of sexuality. A major aim of this work is to help couples get past destructive influences and to grow a healthy synthesis of sexuality and spirituality. To accomplish this we sometimes start by asking a short series of questions designed to be a bit confounding and confusing. With a touch of confusion couples tend to talk longer about the questions and in doing so, they get farther. We vary the questions tailoring them to the couple's background. They usually go something like:

1. Would you feel okay if together you explored the world's many religious traditions which teach that sexuality is spiritual and true spirituality encompasses sexuality?

2. If your religious training was antisexual, will you both make your spirituality prosexual? How?

3. Is your concept of the spiritual or of a higher power (be it nature, the spirit of love in the universe, the Tao, a traditional Jehovah, etc.) understandable as a positive force for sexual pleasure?

4. Together do you dare try to be simultaneously sexual and spiritual?

5. How do you feel talking about these questions with each other?

Jeff answered, "I feel like God is going to zap me dead any minute. My god's a mean, suspicious old man who doesn't want anybody to have any fun." Helen, his wife, retorted, "Since he hasn't zapped us yet, maybe he wants us to have sex." Jeff said, "You mean we don't have to feel guilty every time we want to screw in some new crazy way?" Helen laughed and replied, "No, we might even give thanks for the gifts we are about to receive." Both were sharing the kind of humor that helps shed old programs. Later they read Gillies' book on transcendental sex (1978). In doing the practices suggested, both told of having profound spiritual experiences. Jeff concluded, "It was sex that got me started on being spiritually connected. I got in touch with the awe and the wonder of it all. That really drew Helen and me a lot closer together. It's all so mysterious and incredible. I didn't even know we could have feelings like these. Sharing them with each other is even more awesome."

One authority on codependency and the recovery process put it this way: "If a whole-person recovery is the goal, then it is important to recognize that the sexual embodiment through integrating our intellectual, emotional and physical selves is primary. This can be the beginning of the spiritual dimension of sexuality" (Mason 1988,70).

STARTING YOUR INTEGRATION OF LOVE AND SEX

Do you have enough knowledge about sex? Are you searching for more knowledge? There is always more. Do you have enough knowledge about love? Are you searching for more? Yes, there is lots more even if it is hard to find. Are you and your mate sharing your knowledge about love and sex? Some couples get the knowledge but they are not good at sharing it. Are you and your mate experimenting with how to use your knowledge about sex and love together? Are you developing your teamwork in creating loving sex and sexual loving? If not, get busy. If you get stuck, get help. The brave and the smart do not tolerate staying stuck. By the way, bravery is what you do in spite of fear, not what you do without fear. Now start talking about love and sex to your mate. That is where the integration of love and sex usually starts—with talk.

CoRecovery . . . 9

How Do We Get Off the Codependency Merry-Go-Round?

"It's like we're trapped on a merry-go-round from Hell," Barry said, with utter frustration. "We have the same old ups and downs and we just keep going round and round getting nowhere." Abby, his lover of eight years, added, "Barry's right. We keep saying the same things over and over and we keep having the same old bad feelings we always had. We even have the same old fights." Barry chimed in with, "We both did the same thing with others before we met each other, so I don't think splitting up is the answer." Abby added, "We went to separate counselors for awhile. He got better and I got better, but "we" didn't get better. In fact, at first, counseling just made us go round and round even worse with new topics to feel bad about." "So, Dr. Cookerly," Barry skeptically said, "Can you show us how to get off our merry-go-round?" I told them I believed I could, and with further diagnosis I prescribed the CoRecovery program for them.

With help from their CoRecovery group, Barry and Abby began to build a new teamwork that solved their dilemma. To Barry and Abby, their problems at first seemed more complicated and mysterious than those of other couples in their group. Some couples had simple behavior cycles. The louder Bill got, the louder Cynthia got. The louder Cynthia got, the louder Bill got. Bill and Cynthia had a simple escalation system in which "A" led to "B" and "B" led back to "A." Abby and Barry thought they were lost in something more complicated and confusing.

As Barry and Abby struggled to understand and change their interaction system, they discovered what so many codependent couples do. They had been entangled in the most common of all the patterns that ensnare codependent couples. Abby and Barry were greatly surprised and relieved when they learned their dysfunctional pattern had only three basic parts. What had previously seemed like an endlessly complicated merry-go-round, boiled down to a fairly simple three-part system of interacting. Two things had made this system seem much more complicated. Both

Barry and Abby played all three parts; and they jumped back and forth between the three parts rapidly.

As so often happens in CoRecovery groups, Barry and Abby first saw what they themselves were doing in the simple interaction of another couple named Jane and John.

FROM THE MYSTERIOUS MERRY-GO-ROUND TO THE TREACHEROUS TRIANGLE

Jane, with a disapproving look on her face, complained, "You keep staying away from home longer and longer. You come home from work later and later, and I just hate it." John, her husband, lowered his head and looked downtrodden. Jane continued, "How in the world am I going to get you to come home and be a husband and father like you're supposed to." John sank deeper into his seat and muttered something about being sorry. Jane seeing his demeanor then changed and softly said, "Oh, I didn't mean to hurt your feelings. I'm sorry." John then looked up with an angry sort of expression and said, "You just don't understand how much work it takes to do my job. If you just knew how hard I have to work to support you and the kids, you'd show some appreciation." Jane started to cry saying, "Honey, I do appreciate you, don't be mad, it's okay. I guess I'm just being selfish." Now John looked worried and said, "No, sweetheart, you're right; it's my fault. I need to be a better father." Jane resuming her earlier disapproving look and tone said, "That's right, the children and I need to see more of you." John returned to his downtrodden look. As a couple, they had for the millionth time come full cycle on the destructive *Drama Triangle* that defeats the communications of so many couples.

My group cotherapist asked the couple, "What are you two doing right now?" John dejectedly said, "Same old stuff we always do." Jane looked surprised and said, "Yes, but I'm starting to think I understand, John. I think we are on that Drama Triangle thing that Anna and Bob worked on last week here in couples group."

Barry, the new member of the group asked, "What do you mean by 'Drama Triangle'?"

Andy, another group member said, "Let me try to explain it. It's complicated, but here goes. We codependent couples get trapped into living out a script with only three roles. We switch back and forth between these three roles. The names of the roles are 'victim', 'persecutor' and 'rescuer'. I'm really good at all three roles and so is my wife, Annette. Lots of codependents start out by trying to be rescuers. They end up being victims and persecutors and seldom really rescue anybody."

Annette then added, "I tried to rescue Andy from his cocaine problem. He wasn't ready to be rescued and so I became the victim. As long as he did coke I felt he was persecuting me. Then I got mad and persecuted him for doing coke and for not letting me rescue him. Eventually I'd fall apart and he'd try to rescue me by quitting and being nice. Then I'd pour out all my frustration. I just kept being mad at him. He would go back to coke to hide from my anger and I started trying to rescue him again. We kept doing that sort of thing for years. Then we got into CoRecovery and learned how to get off the Drama Triangle together."

Andy then said, "Annette and I started just like you, in little quick switches between the three roles. Are you starting to see yourselves in this?" Jane and John then began working on their system of interacting. They could see it was filled with Drama Triangle patterns.

Jane told how she felt like a victim when John was absent. She could now see that she depended on him instead of herself to feel safe and okay. In her mind John was supposed to rescue her from all her bad feelings especially those of loneliness and insecurity. She said she never really understood the idea of being responsible for her feelings, but she was beginning to, now.

Jane's way of getting John to rescue her was by persecuting him with shaming statements. She also did this by acting out the role of an unjustly hurt victim. John would, indeed, feel shame and guilt every time she did this. When Jane saw his hurt, she would start to act nice to make him feel better. This rescue effort usually failed. John, instead of acting like a rescued victim, persecuted her for not understanding him. Jane would then return to the victim role and cry a lot. Back and forth they would go. Nothing was ever resolved. They just felt drained and unhappy.

John and Jane worked to identify the statements that represented these roles. "Be a father like you are supposed to," was clearly an attempt to persecute by inducing guilt, as was, "You don't understand how much work it takes me to do my job." Saying, "I'm sorry" and "No, it's my fault, not yours" were rescue efforts. Behaviors like looking downtrodden and crying communicated being in the victim role quite well.

John was the first to discover a disturbing truth. "I do not know any other way to talk to Jane. I want something to change this Drama Triangle stuff, is all I know. We won't have anything to talk about." Jane added, "Yes, what else is there?"

"How can we fix this?" they both asked at once. I said, "Jane, will you ask John for what you really want?" Jane thought a minute, then in a clear, kind voice said, "John, I'd like to see more of you, and right now, I'd like you to reassure me that you're not staying away from me because you don't love me—if that's true. I've been afraid to ask that. That's because it's easy for me to believe no one loves me. This is especially true when I've been playing the victim role. I guess in order to help myself right now, I need to say, 'I'm getting better, and if you don't love me you're missing out on one hell of a fine woman.' There, I feel better already."

John said, "Looking at a strong, okay you, helps me want to be around you more. The truth is, I sometimes stay away because you often seem like a hurt child or my disapproving mom. I've been afraid to tell you that because we get into all that Drama Triangle stuff, and I'm tired of it."

With some additional coaching Jane said, "Suppose we do an experiment. Suppose everyday we both work at greeting each other like okay adults, and show we're glad to see each other." John added, "Okay, I'll come home sooner and I'll come in like a lover instead of like a defensive kid the way I usually do. I do love you even more now seeing your willingness to work on this. It helps me think I've really got to get my part of that triangle stuff out of the way because I see it's standing between us. I have to approach you without the preconceived idea that you are my angry mom or a hurt child; I must really see you instead of my past."

While they were working through all this, Barry asked, "Why is it called the Drama Triangle?" Andy immediately answered, "It's called the Drama Triangle because it's a way to put a lot of drama in our dull, unhappy lives. Like any drama it keeps us distracted from real life and real life's challenges—the ones we codependents keep dodging because we don't think we can handle them. At least that's been true for me." "Yeah, but we're getting the hang of it now, Baby," Annette added as she hugged Andy.

While this is not the historical truth about the term, Drama Triangle, it is a pretty good psychological truth.

John and Jane worked out other details of how they would experiment with new behaviors and help each other to escape the triangle. They slipped back into old behaviors at first, but slowly learned to catch these slips and correct them sooner and sooner in the cycle.

Occupying Two Positions at Once

Codependents, as we have seen, have a compulsion to fix, control and rescue others. This is a way to feel at least a little good about themselves. It is also a way to get and keep a relationship; although subsequently it may not be the relationship the codependent had hoped for. To do this a codependent must find a person who looks like they need fixing, controlling and frequent rescuing, or in other words, a person repeatedly stuck in a victim role. Now two of the three positions on the Drama Triangle have been filled—the rescuer and the victim. So where does the persecutor come in? Well, if you keep needing rescuing I eventually get mad at you for not being "once and for all" rescued, and I begin to persecute you for that. Also you should be a more cooperative and grateful victim, so I am going to let you know how you are failing me. From the other side, if I am a victim wanting to be rescued and you do not do it just right, you are going to hear about it. If I call for help and you do not come quickly enough, that must mean you do not really care enough, right? If you do not show just the right amount of sympathy, take the right amount of time, say just the right things, I'm going to have to test you further to see if you really love me. If you do love me you will rescue me perfectly. Incidently, you have to read my mind to know what I want. If I have to tell you, that spoils it. Don't all fairy tales prove that Prince and Princess Charming always do just the right thing without having to tell each other what they want?

As both the victim and the rescuer I can persecute you. If you need rescuing I can wait longer than you would like. I can also be sure to say things to hurt you as I bail you out, clean up your mess, or do whatever needs to be done to rescue you *again*. As the victim I can persecute you by getting into my next mess when you are at your lowest, in a way that is most embarrassing to you, or at your most inconvenient time *again*. And there are lots of other ways for both the victim and the rescuer to jump into the persecutor role, *again* and *again*.

All this can grow to tragic proportions in codependency. A common example might be: He gets drunk and arrested. She leaves work to bail him out, nurses him over his hangover and then says everything possible to help him feel guilty about it. Then he gets drunk again to get even with her for "guilt tripping" on him. She cries and is so hurt that he starts to comfort her, and the more he comforts the more she cries and complains, until he's the victim planning to get drunk again to escape all the guilt and to get back at her.

Sadly, literally millions of couples waste their relationship lives cycling around and around on this triangle.

Unreal Rescues and Real Life Tragedies

Couples often stay on the Drama Triangle because subconsciously it is a way to live out a role instead of doing real life. You see, most of the rescues are not real. They are only roles we have been programmed to follow. Society programs us with "damsel in distress" and "frog and the princess" stories when we are quite young. Our families often add to this programming by being dysfunctional in ways that promote these scripts. In our secret child self, when we feel unloved and do not feel great about ourselves, we can think, "If I save someone they'll love me," or "If someone saves me that means they care." So we get into these rescuer and victim roles. Then we get frustrated because it never really works. In our frustration we become persecutors of those we think are sabotaging the happy endings. Subconsciously we become the victim having learned that someone will rescue us. Or subconsciously we can pick victims for relationships so we can be the hero or heroine. It seems so safe to play hero instead of being a champion of developing democratic, well-functioning teamwork.

The trouble is when we live on the triangle we dodge real life. By doing so we and the relationship deteriorate. In a twisted way it is so interesting and captivating to be caught-up in this dramatic, albeit ruinous, living. Living on the triangle is an escapist route, to avoid developing adult-to-adult relationships.

The Drama Triangle is dramatic and interesting until reality tragically intervenes. He gets drunk and dies. She overdoses and her brain never really works right again. He gets tired of it and leaves her for a better "mommy" (caretaker). She finds a better "big daddy" (rescuer). Either one of them may individually enter treatment, grow up enough and, sadly, leave their mate behind and abandoned. Then the untreated mate may find someone new to start the cycle again. All too often they sink farther into their destructive existence. Sometimes they learn and grow out of it the second or third time around, and sometimes not.

If both enter couples treatment together, they both can learn to grow more self-dependent and healthfully interdependent. Consequently, they become far better at adult teamwork. Even if the couple finds divorce to be their healthiest choice, they can (in couples treatment) become far better equipped for their next relationship, and can better coparent if there are children to raise.

Real Rescue or the Drama Triangle?

In real rescues the rescuer seldom forms a relationship with the victim. The fireman usually doesn't marry the person he or she saves from the burning building, but might suggest adherence to fire safety codes. The nurse generally doesn't end up in bed with the patient she or he nurses back to health, but might suggest a handbook for learning better health and self-care. The lifeguard seldom falls in love with the person he or she pulls out of the water, but might strongly recommend swimming lessons. The psychotherapist rarely marries the patient, but might stress learning self-rescuing and self-care. Healthy, real love relationships are formed with people who can be or become equal partners, not people enacting parent and child roles forever.

In the next group session John and Jane contracted with each other for a seven-day experimental period. They planned to keep daily notes on how well they did at recognizing their Drama Triangle patterns. They would also note how well they did at substituting new healthy behaviors. The following week they reported that four of the seven days were pretty bad. However, they said the good days were so good that they would extend their experiment and give themselves another chance with this new teamwork. A month later they reported that the new way of greeting each other after work was really working. The most amazing thing was that John had arrived home before Jane three out of seven days. Jane and John went on to tackle even more difficult Drama Triangle patterns; in about three months they told their couples group that they thought they had stopped cycling on the Drama Triangle. They said they had the tools to escape the triangle if they found their behavior slipping backwards. They also felt proud; a new intimacy had developed because they were doing it together.

The Drama Triangle was first identified in ancient Greek theater, thousands of years ago. To create an absorbing drama, Aeschylus began the style of dramatic tragedy in which there were three main roles—victim, persecutor, and rescuer. Greek theater has always been a great reflector of real human experience.

I was first introduced to the concept of the Drama Triangle in a workshop conducted by Dr. Eric Bern and his associates. Dr. Bern was the founder of the form of therapy know as Transactional Analysis or T.A. In T.A. it was called a "game," played quite commonly in an alcoholic's relationships (1964, 1988). Right away I could identify with what he was saying. In my own life I saw what a rescuer I was. My two alcoholic parents took a lot of rescuing; so did several of my early "love" interests. Naturally, when these young women would not be rescued properly, I slipped into feeling hopelessly trapped in the victim position. When I got tired of feeling hopeless, I'd get mad, just like my dad used to do, and verbally persecute them in Olympic style. As soon as they looked hurt enough, I'd start rescuing again. It took a lot of work for me to learn how to act in ways that promote only self-rescue. I also had to learn not to punish others if they weren't doing it "right" which, of course, just meant "my way."

Self-Rescuing Couples Versus Learned Helplessness

Rescues can help people learn to be helpless. It is important to know that when you act to rescue a person without their self-rescuing coequal action, you help them to feel powerless and unable to depend on themselves. If this becomes a fixed mind-set, self-confidence, self-esteem, and most important of all, healthy self-love may be seriously depleted. This sets the stage for a downward spiral, which in a mated relationship guarantees eventual failure. The failure may take the form of an ongoing mutual misery marriage, divorce, escape into addiction, escape by illness or sudden abandonment (possibly via suicide). Living on the triangle always eventually fails. If there are children before the final failure occurs, they are usually programmed to carry out their relationships in the same way.

Curing this problem means learning to work as a team of equals, where no one has to live in a "one down" position.

George said, "Mary, I'm starting to feel a little like a victim again because we're not being as sexual as I'd like." Mary responded, "I feel a little attacked and maybe a bit hurt by the way you said that. I wonder if you would be willing to start over and say that another way?" "Sure." George said, "I think I might feel attacked too, if you had said to me what I just said to you, now that I think about it. Let's see, how about, 'Mary, let's start being more sexual, I think we are slipping a little in that department.' Was that better?" Mary said, "Okay, George, that's fine if you're also willing to be a little bit more loving with me. I'm feeling like I want to be told what you appreciate about me and I'd like to be cuddled more." George smiled and said, "Sounds great to me. I could use that, too. Let's start tonight as soon as we get home from this counseling session."

This is a couple who has learned to catch their Drama Triangle behaviors early. They have learned to love themselves well enough not to be easily threatened by what the other one says. They have also learned to go into the future tense when talking about what they are going to jointly do about a difficulty. They used to get endlessly lost analyzing and disagreeing about who did what. How it is going to be fixed is a lot more important than whose fault it is. George and Mary have also learned how to ask for what they want directly instead of blaming (persecutor) each other for what they are not getting (victim), or feeling responsible for what the other one is not getting (rescuer). They used to be able to drag out their old drama, about not getting enough sex or love, to three weeks of escalating misery. According to their estimates they occasionally slip back and do their old pattern for about twenty minutes, max. Now they can quickly return to doing a lot of love and sex whenever they slip and allow their busy lives to get them off track.

It is more an act of caring to help a person learn to rescue themselves than to do it for them. Our society has glorified the rescuer role. I worked my way through college partly by being a lifeguard and swimming teacher. I learned that teaching swimming is a lot more fun. Lifeguarding is very restrictive: always having to be ready to rescue, watching others have fun playing in the water but not being able to play in it myself. Being confined to the heroic watcher position is quite lonely. Worst of all, when I had to really rescue someone I was in danger of being dragged down too. When I pulled somebody out of the water the most they ever did was say "Thank You" and go away. Then I'd just go back on guard. Later I had to learn not to behave like a lifeguard in my mated love relationships. Finally I found an "excellent swimmer"; this woman could take care of herself. Now I could just "play in the water" with her.

The Drama Triangle way of doing a mated relationship can be played out in large and small ways. She gets drunk and nearly dies and he gets her to the hospital again. He loses all their money gambling, and she takes a second job to pull them through. Tragic, life-destroying dramas are all too common. More subtle is the constant, petty problems route. He is never happy with his job, and she is always trying to create a new solution for him, which he never tries. She is never happy with her mother and he is always advising her on how to fix it, but it never fixes. Large scale or small scale, couples can learn the adult-to-adult teamwork it takes to stop living this way and get on to a loving life. This is one of my great rewards in life: I get to see so many couples go on to love-filled, real living. You can too.

CoRecovery . . . 10

How Do We Travel the Path of Ongoing Love?

Are you making mated love an adventure to be lived or is it just problems to be solved? Is mated love increasingly like a jointly traveled journey or is it only a lonely, hoped for destination? Does mated love mean sharing feelings of all kinds or is it feeling emotionally walled out or in? As we learn to travel the path of love together we can learn how to achieve the best that love has to offer. To do this we have to learn how to stay on the path of CoRecovery. Setbacks will occur. When they do, the challenge of CoRecovery is to regain the path of ongoing love. Accomplishing this takes facing some additional issues and acquiring some additional skills.

LOVE CENTERING AND RECENTERING

To keep on, or return to, the path of ongoing love, it is important to learn how to "center in love." We humans can center in many things besides love. It is common for codependents to center in rescuing, controlling, or safety actions. Some center in anger, despair, and anxiety. Others let things like addictions, jealousy, and possessiveness dominate the center of their being. There are also people who center themselves in power, money, or status. Being right, righteous, or rebellious is at the center of many other people's behaviors. Whatever we put at the center of our focus that is not love, can make us lose sight of love. Whatever we let be at the center of our reason for being can displace healthful love from our emotional center. Whenever love is not at our center our love relationships can suffer loss, even profound loss.

Lewis said, "I used to center on winning. The trouble was every time 'I' won, 'we' lost. Whenever I won an argument Paula felt like a loser and there was less love between us. Now I know to say to myself, 'Lewis, Old Boy, you had better center yourself in love; you're after winning again.

Love yourself but also love Paula.' Every time I recenter like this my attitude improves and Paula senses it. I still go after what I think is right but I'm a lot more loving when I do it."

Paula then told how she centers herself in love. "I take a big slow breath. Then I do some self-talk. I say, 'Anger, I'm not going to let you be my center. Frustration and despair, you don't get to take me over either. Martyrdom habits, get out of my head. Love, come and be my center at this difficult time. I'm going to come from love toward Lewis and toward myself.' Then I talk to Lewis. When we 'lose it' we take time-outs. Sometimes we forget but we eventually remember what works. And then we turn our childish arguments into adult discussions."

This ability to recenter in love is an acquired habit. Slowly the love-centering habit displaces the older habits of centering in dysfunctional behaviors. It takes an incredible amount of work. The only thing I know that takes more work in a relationship is the emotional energy, wasted time and futile effort of *not* centering in love. So, to regain and to stay on the path of ongoing love, learning to center in love is an excellent skill to acquire. By the way, if the love is all sacrificial, it is not centered. Remember, giving all your love away to others with none for yourself is not loving others as you love yourself. Unless there is an urgent emergency, truly requiring sacrifice, love centering includes being good to yourself. Breathing deeply, quietly telling the hurt parts of yourself loving messages, giving yourself a pat on the back are all ways to begin. Dr. Irene Kassorla, a famous relationship therapist, achieved great success with her "give yourself a kiss" approach (1976).

FOR LOVE'S SAKE, KEEP YOUR SELF-DEPENDENCE

Kahlil Gibran, the great philosopher-poet, probably said it best when writing of mated love; the Prophet says:

> ". . . let there be spaces in your togetherness,
> And let the winds of the heavens dance between you.
> Love one another but make not a bond of love:
> Let it rather be a moving sea between the shores of your souls.
> Fill each other's cup but drink not from one cup.
> Give one another of your bread but eat not from the same loaf" (1923, 16-17).

To stay on the path of ongoing mate love, it is best if both partners keep developing their individuality. When loving mates have new ideas to share, new playful and loving ways to interact, and they go into new experiences together, the relationship is constantly renewed. Neither is dependent on the other for vitality. Both contribute from their individuality to the whole. This is a synergistic process contributing to the vitality of the relationship.

Conversely, when we act to inhibit each other's growth or inhibit our individual growth, the relationship suffers. Usually this is done out of fear. When I fear your growth will take you from me, or show me up, I may work against your growth. When I do this I work against our relationship because I am letting fear win over love. When I inhibit growth, yours, mine, or ours, I act in support of dependency and the stagnation and deterioration it brings. To love you well, I must make love more important than fear. If I do that, my actions support your growth as an individual. The more you become, the more you have to share and the same is true of me. From the sharing of our individual growth flows the growth of our relationship.

Enhanced and lovingly shared individuality is a primary defense against enmeshment and codependency itself. In fact it can be seen as the exact opposite of a codependent relationship. One of the most important findings in the studies of how healthy relationships differ from dysfunctional ones concerns the enhancement of individuality. Healthy relationships encourage, support and promote the process of becoming increasingly the individual you are capable of becoming (Lewis *et al* 1976). Unhealthy relationships promote the loss of individuality and increase enmeshment and codependence.

Codependency problems tend to keep reoccurring until couples become proficient at extending their individuality and sharing it. To accomplish the sharing component requires a combination of self-disclosure loving and affirmational loving. As we grow individually we self-disclose our growth. As our mate's growth is disclosed to us, we must appreciate and affirm them for their growth. If instead we threaten ourselves with our mate's growth, we temporarily can fall back on tolerational loving, while we work on self-love. When our self-love is great enough, we tend not to threaten ourselves with our mate's growth. When we do get stuck in a rut and aren't growing, we may become insecure and want our mates to quit growing and expanding their experiences. When we depend on ourselves to keep growing, and we share our growth, we stay on the path of ongoing love.

One of the exercises we use in CoRecovery couples counseling is especially designed to assist this process. Couples can do it at home. We instruct the couples to sit facing each other, hold one hand and slowly read each of the following statements to each other. After each statement we ask them to look into each other's eyes for about ten seconds and mentally focus on what is being said. The statements go like this:

- When we make more of ourselves individually, we can be more together.
- You must improve in your way and I must improve in my way. When we lovingly share our improvements, we together improve.
- When I act to inhibit your growth, I act to inhibit our growth.
- When I refuse to improve or reject your improvements, our improvement is hindered.
- When I surrender my growth or growth opportunities, or ask you to surrender yours, we move toward being less.
- When you are more, and when I am more and we lovingly share, we are more.
- Become all that you can be, my love. Become who you really are and not a mere copy of who I would have you be.
- Share the real and the growing you, and I will strive to do the same. In the sharing I hope to love the real you, and perhaps you will love the real me. Then we can grow our love together.

Couples have varied reactions to this exercise. Some couples smile and hold each other. Some are upset and argue. Others denounce these ideas. Some couples are silent and often puzzled. And others get confused, go into denial, or forget. Many couples state they feel loved, close, accepted, and understood. Some couples later say they are thankful for what they gained from the exercise. Most couples have a better hold on how improving their self-growth and self-dependence improves their love relationship.

FOR LOVE'S SAKE, GROW YOUR INTERDEPENDENCE

Teamwork and interdependence mean about the same thing. Good teams are always working to improve their teamwork. Improvements in teamwork are always possible. Good team members consistently work on two things. The first is improving themselves individually. The second is improving their cooperative interaction with the rest of their team.

The family I grew up in was terrible at teamwork. Consequently, my parents were defeated by the challenges and issues which accompanied recurring alcoholism, violence, and poverty. Most of all they were defeated by not knowing how to effectively show the love they felt. I grew up thinking teamwork meant "get control" or "be controlled." But later I ran into a great example of teamwork; in high school I became a member of a notably weak football team. The newspaper said we would finish last in the city; we were the lightest and smallest team. We were slow; we didn't have a single star or even any near-star. Everyday our coaches shouted the challenge at us, "You're small, you're slow and you're not stars. Your only hope is teamwork." And we believed them. In preseason we lost all but one game, and in losing, we really learned teamwork. In the regular season we won every game. On teamwork alone we became the city champs. It took the state champs to finally beat our "no speed, no big guys, no stars" teamwork. If only my parents had known what the word teamwork really meant what a difference it would have made in all our lives. Later I learned how this same teamwork saved lives in hospitals, made dysfunctional families functional, and was crucial to couples. I also learned how to do it in my love life.

In good interdependence we are always improving our "contracts" and our negotiating skills. The process is not always pleasant—we hassle, we grump, and we gripe. But with good democratic interaction and teamwork we style and restyle our contracts as conditions change. We can trust that we will, to the best of our ability, fulfill the contract, but we also know it will be done imperfectly. When there is a failure we renegotiate. This is a never-ending process and we know it. We also know that if we have to, we can take over the functions of our mate; our self-dependence will see us through. Knowing my mate can accomplish things for herself helps me respect her. Knowing she agrees sometimes to depend on me, but does not have to, helps me respect myself as someone who can be depended upon. Knowing that my mate can live without me, but chooses not to, helps me respect our relationship. Out of our chosen interdependence, we stay on the path of ongoing love.

Free-Gift Love and The Natural Child

A small child delights in drawing on a piece of paper. Suddenly, the child darts over to you and gives you the gift so diligently worked on. Before you have the chance to offer thanks, the child is back at work on the next creation. Most people who deal with children experience this natural expression of material loving. The child found joy in the creating and giving of the love. The gift was not made and given to get love in return. It was a free gift—no strings attached.

Deep inside us lives our natural child-self. Our natural self can love in this free gift, nonmanipulative way. Codependency contaminates real love with manipulations. As we grow free of codependency we can increasingly give love because it feels good to do so. Sidney Mellon in his extensive anthropological investigation into the evolution of human love discovered some surprising things. In both primitive human cultures and primate groups around the world free gift love behaviors occur (1981). In fact, of the many types of mammals who live in groups that have been studied in the wild, most demonstrate what can be called free gift behaviors. In medical sociology, research indicates that people who enjoy behaving with altruistic love (free gift love) live longer and healthier (Selye 1976).

To keep on the path of ongoing love we need to keep in touch with our natural child self, who will help us enjoy the gift of giving love. The sheer freedom of giving love without regard to what we get in return leads to pure joy.

Love and Ever-Varying Emotional Intercourse

Jessy was emphatic, "Sexual intercourse can be positively great but emotional intercourse is ten times better." Katrina, Jessy's mate, vigorously disagreed, "Emotional intercourse is only three or four times as great as sexual intercourse." Jessy said with a wink, "Let's go home and experiment. I'm sure I can prove it to you." Katrina raised an eyebrow and added, "I'm willing to be proven wrong."

As couples continue to grow, they find new feelings to share. Many people are surprised that there are feelings they may not have experienced or shared. Do you know what it is like to feel and share the somewhat rare emotions of blitheness, glee, wonder, preciousness, titillation, concord, fervor, mellowness, rapture, commitment, amiability, ardor, carefree, buoyancy, jauntiness, belonging, exaltation, and reverence, to name but a few? If not you have a lot to look forward to. These feelings are adult elaborations of simpler states of feeling good. Couples who continue to grow can keep making these adult elaborations and develop a very rich life together. Many couples quit after reaching a plateau of feeling less pain and some simple joys. Others go for more, for natural highs. For continued growth why not go for all you can get and share? Sharing has a way of doubling any good feeling. Emotional intercourse is something you can always vary in new and different ways. Between both sexual and emotional intercourse, you cannot get around to all that is healthfully possible in your lifetime, but you and your love mate can sure try.

LOVE MODELING FOR CHILDREN

How did you see adults show each other love as you grew up? What you saw was a model for you. That modeling built a program in the computer-like parts of your brain to do what you saw your parents do about love in adulthood. Luckily we have other parts of the brain that are curious and look for new and better ways. We also have a natural love hunger drive operating within us. So if you did not have all of the eight major ways people can love each other modeled for you, you can learn them. As you learn them you can model them for your children. Then they will have a head start on love and all its benefits in their lives.

In modeling love for children you will probably have to overcome two or more sets of programs in your head. One set of programs comes from your society or culture, the other from your family-of-origin. We are just beginning to see that our cultural programs can be just as influential as our family's.

Multicultural perspectives are beginning to have a strong influence on how professionals counsel clients (Pederson 1991). When it comes to modeling love for children we see many of the non-English speaking peoples do it better. This is especially true of modeling tactile love among adults. Hugs, pats, cuddles, holding and all the rest have been deemed sinfully sexual in more segments of English speaking countries than in the rest of the Western world. This prohibition against loving touch often leads to touch deprivation. As we have already mentioned, loving touch is instrumental in triggering a host of healthy chemical reactions in the body.

All too many families and cultures model against the major forms of showing love. In these it is not okay to say "I love you" or expressively show it, to affirm someone's importance, to declare how you really feel, or anything else that might demonstrate love. Material gifts are about the only acceptable way to show love among many elements of society. Our culture models hate and indifference far better than it models love. According to one broad, extensive cultural comparison, societies that insufficiently model love weaken themselves until they are destroyed. This study suggests that this will be our culture's fate unless we become much more love-oriented and love-demonstrative. In this same research, it was found that our society promotes only one type of situation in which love is acceptable for adults; it was called "refuge love." (Fine 1985)

The idea is that in order to get acceptable love in our culture we have to get in such bad shape as to need refuge. Then it is okay for adults to show each other love. For many, if your mate just died, I can give you a little pat at the funeral. If you learn you have cancer, you might accept a comforting hug. That is the way many of us grew up. When children grow up watching adults be love stingy, love awkward, and love rejecting, they tend to do the same thing when they become adults.

Because of sex prohibitions it is likely you have at least some cultural programming to reduce your demonstration of love to other adults when children appear. That is probably what you watched happen when you were growing up. You even watched it on TV and in the movies.

You also may have some subconscious programming that taught you to get in a mess because it is a way to get refuge love. Our refuge love training is unfortunately a great promoter of codependence. If I stay weak, sick, need rescuing, and generally dependent, maybe you will give me refuge love. If I get okay society has taught me maybe no one will show me love. Even if someone does, as a strong, independent, individual, I must reject demonstrations of love to prove my adequacy. I must also show my children this is "the thing to do." We must especially show this to boys so they can grow up to be cold, calculating warriors. We do this too well—look at the violence in our society. Tragically, this training is a way to destroy our children's future at love. Model tough, insensitive indifference today and tomorrow you may watch your children go from one love-starved relationship to another. Model lots of adult-to-adult love and they have a chance to do much better.

To stay on the path of ongoing love, it is important not to stop showing love when children are around. A solid majority of people afflicted with codependence say, "I never saw my parents hug" or "I seldom heard my parents say, 'I love you' to each other." Will your children say the same thing? And will their children? You can break the loveless chain.

Far too many couples in trouble report things started going wrong when the children came along. Tracing the origins of the pattern often leads to a surprise for many couples. As the children matured the parents stopped showing each other love. Further examination usually shows the grandparents did the same thing. The older the children got the more the parents did not show each other love.

Loretta said, "It just didn't feel right hugging or kissing my husband in front of the kids when they were small. Now they blame us for their hang-ups about showing love."

Maria said, "I'm so fortunate I grew up in an Italian home where there was lots of love shown—tender, boisterous, sexy, sweet, sad, every kind of love. My parents, all my aunts and uncles, everybody loved everybody and showed it every day. Then I married Nathaniel. He was raised a real Puritan. After the lights were out, he was great. But in front of others, nothing. That's part of why I left him. Our kids are still young and I don't want them to grow up inhibited and stiff about love. It took the shock of the kids and I moving out for Nathaniel to start trying. Maybe we'll get back together and maybe we won't, but at least we are in counseling together, and dating again."

Staying on the path of ongoing love means showing love everywhere. In some public and social settings, demonstrations of love may be more subtle and subdued. At home in front of children, avoid blatant expressions of sexual love. Partly, that's because children may only see and be confused by the sexuality and not see the love in such occurrences. It is the love children need to see. In public it is good for children to see that adults can hug each other, friends can openly appreciate one another, and adults can give and receive love in all its eight major forms. These demonstrations are more common in much of the Western world. You can model love and help your children live in a better world. By doing so you will also be helping yourselves stay on the path of ongoing love.

LOVE IN BREAKUPS AND DIVORCES

Ada said, "We have solved all our problems, we get along great and we have decided to get a divorce." "Why?" everyone said at once. Byron said, "We figured out we love each other like a brother and a sister love each other, not like mates. So we want the group's help with transition." "We plan to always be active in each others' lives," Ada added. Byron went on, "We deeply and sincerely love each other better than we ever have. This CoRecovery group has worked wonders for us. Without it, we'd be getting a messy divorce like our friends, one full of hostility and strife." Ada then rather angrily said, "My sister and her ex fell into the American divorce trap. They let their lawyers pit them against each other. They had a long knock-down-drag-out legal fight. Then the lawyers took a third of their money, went home, and forgot them. My sister, her ex and their kids have been terribly hurt by the way that divorce went down, and I don't think they ever will get over it.

Byron and I are not going to let anyone do that to us. Crazy as it sounds, we are going to have a loving divorce." Byron nodded, then gave Ada a little squeeze and quipped, "Anyone know a preacher who does divorce ceremonies? This decision is so right we simply must invite all our friends." Ada laughed and joked, "I wonder if Ms. Manners knows what color my dress should be?" Ada and Byron went on to work out a very healthy divorce. Some of their family members tried to play a mind game called, "Let's you two fight and we'll pick sides," but Byron and Ada did not let them. They were positively brutal with their attorneys; they set the limits and made it perfectly clear that every negotiation would be fair and friendly. They do seem to be living something like "happily ever after"—apart.

Well-planned divorces and breakups may not all go as well as Byron and Ada's. However, they can go a lot better than our culture's patterns for divorce. For a long time now, we have known that a counseled divorce is a healthier divorce (Brown 1970; Cookerly 1976).

One of the most poignant things I ever heard about a divorce came from an intelligent teenager. Her parents had been engaged in a long, drawn out, destructive divorce process. She and her parents had been ordered to family counseling to see if the destructiveness could at least be reduced. In the course of one family session, she asked to read from a letter she had written to her parents. In quiet, measured tones she read:

"I'm very angry with both of you, not for divorcing but for divorcing this way. It's obvious to me you know nothing about love. The way you are fighting over me proves that. In fact the way you are going about this divorce proves to me you never really loved each other. I don't know what you felt, but it couldn't have been love. People who were once in love would never treat each other like you two do. You both say you love me. Does that mean that someday you will treat me like you're treating each other right now? Your war with each other has made me lose all respect for you, and as far as I'm concerned, the sooner I don't have to have anything to do with either of you, the better."

This honest statement did trigger a big change. Both parents were able to see they were overly invested in controlling the outcome of the divorce, and manipulating their daughter away from the other parent. Slowly, they made a respectable peace. Slowly, they healed the relationship with their daughter. Slowly, they put at least a modicum of love into their outcome. They found it better to be coparents instead of combatants.

Divorces and breakups do not have to mean the end of ongoing love. In today's world if you divorce, or end a mated love relationship, you do not have to do it destructively. Increasing numbers of ex's remain (or become) real friends, enjoy seeing each other on holidays, and healthfully love each other.

If You Lose the Path, Look for Love-Centered Allies

Long before anyone seriously takes action to breakup or divorce I strongly suggest finding some love-centered support. In a world that needs to be more love-oriented, it takes some work to find love-oriented people, but it can be done. When you lose the path of love, people who are on the path are the best ones to help you find it again. Shame induces codependent people to hide their problems from others. Also, the codependent person desires to be the caretaker, be in control, be the fixer and not the fixed, and that leads to isolation. This isolation makes a person more love hungry. Isolation worsens the couple's problems. Seeking out allies who model how to live a more love-filled life will alleviate that isolation. Here are five guidelines to use in identifying good love allies:

1. When you talk with a potential ally, do you usually come away feeling nurtured, cared about and energized? Do you also feel better about yourself or at least less bad? If you do, that probably means you received some human-to-human love. With more love inside, you can deal better with yourself and your mate. If these things are true you and your mated relationship may have found a good love ally.

2. When you talk with a potential love ally, does it seem like you are being dealt with truthfully? A good love ally will not just appease you, side with you, or tell you what you want to hear. When you get off the path of ongoing love, a good love ally helps you know that both you and your mate need to improve, not just your mate. We all need truth lovingly presented, not just one-sided support. A good love ally uses these two major tools together: love and truth. There are those whose truth is brutal and unloving. There are those whose love is not insightful. Love without truth will not feed your mind. Truth without love will not feed your spirit.

3. A good love ally will love inclusively, not exclusively. This means your ally will be for, not against, your mate. Good love allies join with you against the problems, not against your mate. When you are helped to go against anyone, you are helped to go farther from the path of ongoing love. Time and time again I have seen people told to view their mate as the wrong-doer, the sinner, the sick one and other derisive names that force people apart. In time, this training in scornful exclusion always does more harm than good. A good love ally works for the benefit of all concerned. They will side with you against your difficulties, but not against your mate, relatives, offspring, friends or anyone else.

4. A good love ally champions a healthy relationship outcome. Some people are blindly on the side of breaking up while others are blindly on the side of staying together. I once heard a father tell his daughter, "I don't care how many times he puts you in the hospital, your duty is to stay with your husband." I asked him if the God he believed in could be against his daughter's physical health and survival. He adamantly replied that staying dutifully married was more important. I told him as a health specialist, I could not agree. His daughter's husband, however, was on the side of her well-being. He told her, "Until I get my temper

under control, stay away from me. If I can't do that, I would rather have you divorced than dead." He was, in my view, starting to be a better love ally than her father.

Some people are subconsciously for everyone breaking up. Their efforts at mated love have not done well. They may want to watch you go through a divorce. If you fare well, they may follow. Others are in the misery-loves-company group. There are those who are envious. Others are jealous and want a chance at your mate. Even more want to live vicariously through your struggles. A few may be your secret enemies and want to see you brought down. Still others may want you free so they can have a chance at you.

There is one particularly large group who subconsciously want you and your mate to fail; they are people in denial about their need to improve at love. If there are people all around them failing at love, they won't stand out as inadequate. Another group is more benign. The only way they know how to be on your side is to be against your relationship. Quite often they are still thinking like a child about mated love. They may naively tell you that your troubles mean your relationship is not right for you and you should find someone else. "When you find Mr. or Ms. Right, everything will magically go right" sums up their unenlightened understanding of love. Good love allies know that the best of relationships have problems, struggles and issues to face. In speaking of his marriage, a sea-faring captain once told his CoRecovery group, "There are no long journeys without storms to weather, and unless this ship of ours is really sunk, I'm not about to abandon it."

5. Good love allies usually do well in their love relationships. A good love ally may have lost at love, but they learn from it and go on to win at love. They are likely to have deep solid family, friend, mate and self-love. One or more of these love relationships may be absent but not all of them. Love allies are themselves on the path of ongoing love most of the time. They may have lost and regained the path and in doing so, know more about staying on it than you do. I once asked a man facing his third divorce where he got his knowledge about how love works. "In places where there are a lot of people professing to know a lot about love," he said. "Where is that?" I asked. "In bars full of divorced drunks," he laughingly admitted. Then he added, "I think I ought to try another group. Right? But where should I look?"

Well, here are seven places to look. But keep in mind the five guidelines given above. First, take a look at your family. You may have one or more family members who can make a good love ally. Some people have been so hurt in their families that they overlook an aunt or uncle, a parent who has improved, a sister or brother who is growing, or a cousin who always seemed to care. You already have a basis for relating to your family members. In all relationships, there are dangers. Your family-of-origin may represent too much danger, but don't count them out without considering them. Think about each member separately. Consider them in relation to the love ally criteria. If you still are not sure, talk to them about each of the five ideas. See how you feel and think about your conversation with them on these issues. If it is good, go on. If not, look elsewhere.

The second place to look for love allies is among your friends and acquaintances. The same precautions that apply to family members apply here. "My best friend always ends up in bed with my mate" doesn't mean abandon friendship, but rather choose friends more wisely. Another statement sometimes made is, "I don't have any real friends, only acquaintances." An acquaintance is a potential friend. Start with some self-disclosure. Confess a problem to see if you feel cared about. If not, check out someone else.

Some people say, "I don't like my friends or my acquaintances." Well, then, you have to look for new people to put in your life. People similar to yourself often make the best potential friends. To find people similar to yourself go where people have interests similar to your own. It is best if your mate will go, too. Those who befriend you both are more likely to be good love allies to your relationship. Friendship love is among the most important kinds of love we can experience. Friendship love is much undervalued in our culture. Real friends will stick by you whether you and your mate break up or not. If your friendship network is all couples or all singles, something may be wrong. It may be a mutual protection society instead of a network of truly loving friends. Real friendship is all-weather love. It is not just fair weather or just foul weather.

Another place to look for love allies who can help you find and stay on the path of love can be called a spiritual fellowship. Now check yourself and see what kind of emotional reaction you are having to the words, "spiritual fellowship." Are you having any negative feelings? Perhaps you are thinking, "I should do that" but you know you don't want to. Honor those feelings; they are probably telling you, you might find yourself in a nonloving or even antilove religious group. You may have been exposed to empty, shallow or even abusive religion. That suggests you may not have been exposed to healthful spiritual people. You certainly will not need guilt-based religion. Love-based spirituality is a whole different thing.

Possibly you are feeling anger. Honor those feelings. They are trying to make you powerful enough to reject what may be a bad idea for you. Unhealthy attempts at spirituality are definitely to be avoided. If you are mostly curious or hopeful start looking for a healthy spiritual fellowship. The same five guidelines definitely apply. Wonderful love allies can be found among healthy people who seek to grow spiritually. If you search broadly, you will find a spiritual home. One man defiantly said, "If you can send us to a church where I don't have to believe in somebody else's God, where they are not against sex, where they do not brainwash you with dogma, and where we are free to say what we really think, I'll go." He was surprised to hear a host of responses from his CoRecovery group members. "Try the Unitarians." "Go Sufi dancing." "Visit my Twelve Step group." "You'll feel okay enough with the Presbyterians." "Have you done a sweat with the Native American Church—the one the Indians started?" "We'll take you to our temple—you'll be amazed." "Our Tai Chi class has a wonderful spiritual philosophy. Want to go with us?" He replied, "I don't know what even half of those things are." His mate said, "I don't either but I'm game; let's go find out." Last I heard they were feeling pretty good with a Methodist couples group. There are many healthy love-centered groups to be found in traditional religious settings as well as in the more unconventional. You and your mate must explore and evaluate to find a group with potential love allies in a spiritual setting.

One of the best love allies you can find is a good love-centered counselor or therapist. Whenever there is a love problem, a loving and love knowledgeable therapist can be of enormous help. As before, the five guidelines apply. If you do not come away from a counseling session feeling cared about and truthfully dealt with, look for another counselor. If you feel your counselor is taking sides talk to your counselor about it, but if you continue to sense inequality you may need someone else. If your counselor is for the healthy outcome of your relationship and not for or against it, per se, you are probably doing well. It doesn't hurt to question counselors about their love failures and successes. If it seems a therapist is succeeding at love, that therapist is likely to be a good love ally. Unfortunately, there are counselors and therapists who haven't even begun to succeed at love. They may be good at dealing with one type of problem or another, but if yours is a love-related problem, you will probably need a love successful ally.

Another great place to find love allies is in a support group. Twelve Step groups can be great and so can others. Support groups for couples can sometimes be found through churches, synagogues, and other religious fellowships. Marriage encounter and couples enrichment organizations also offer couples support groups. It is important to know that support groups are not therapy groups. A good support group does what the word says, it supports. If a couple needs support for coping, adjusting, staying in recovery and finding again the path of ongoing love they will do well to find such a group. While support groups offer many benefits they are quite different from modern group counseling and group therapy. The most obvious difference is that support groups are self-run and therapy groups are facilitated by professionals.

Once again the same five criteria apply in finding love allies in support groups. Members of some support groups play destructive psychological games. Sitting around and bad-mouthing mates, parents or others who are not present is of little help. Playing "pathology," where we endlessly discuss what is wrong, but never get into how to make it right is of little assistance. Playing "ain't it awful" and "let's all just feel sorry for one another" won't really accomplish much either. Good support groups encourage healthy, real progress and don't encourage game playing. Some people are forming CoRecovery support groups for couples. Sometimes out of couple's retreats, workshops and seminars an ongoing support group may be formed. Ministers, priests, rabbis, counselors and treatment centers often know of such groups or are willing to help start them.

Couples group counseling and couples group therapy provide another place for finding good love allies for relationships. Good group therapy will offer the same things as a support group, plus a whole lot more. Modern group therapy can provide techniques for profound healing, for overcoming obstacles and for a couple's growth and development. Most people in CoRecovery groups report that their group provided excellent love allies.

When there are severe problems associated with codependency psychiatric hospitalization may be necessary. A good hospital program brings out the best in people; the worst may also come out but can be expertly dealt with in a safe environment. Often when the best comes out the patients and staff form a love-oriented community. In such a community patients can learn to gain and maintain several kinds of love. Healthy self-love, friendship love and family love are being worked on in most modern psychiatric settings. Recently, with the addition of CoRecovery and similar programs, direct work on mate love is also being included. There are, however, psychiatric facilities that offer little or no help for healthy love development. In these facilities the staff may be made up of people who are not love focused or love knowledgeable, the program may be loveless, or the hospital may center on profit and have an aura of indifference masked as professionalism. Or it may be an institution centered so totally on its bureaucratic rules that love-centered therapy cannot thrive. A love-responsive staff is very important for a love-helpful program. The same five guidelines apply to a hospital staff. In a good full-care program a patient's mate and family are included; loved ones are increasingly being cared for in treatment. A couple's program for treating relationship problems is in evidence. I have worked in, and consulted at, a lot of hospitals. Invariably the good ones are places of loving care. Great love allies can be found in such places.

WHEN THERE ARE SEVERE PERSONAL PROBLEMS

Sometimes one or both mates has a severe difficulty. Life-threatening illnesses, severely debilitating accidents, or diseases and catastrophic loss all provide intense stressors to mated relationships. Among these can be pronounced brain disorders, severe mental and emotional conditions and advanced levels of substance addictions. I like to suggest that couples facing such problems include couples counseling as part of their strategy. This is particularly true for couples afflicted with codependency. All too often such relationships either fall apart under the stress of the severe problem or soon after the problem is solved. To guard against such dangers, learning to apply love while under stress can be a life-rescuing and relationship-saving endeavor—the more love the better. I remember one grateful lady who thanked me by saying, "We wouldn't have made it when our daughter died if it weren't for couples counseling." In severe difficulties individual problems sometimes have to be addressed first, with CoRecovery work following. Whenever possible, I recommend mixing the two. Activating the couple's eight major ways of showing love and the teamwork approaches often greatly increases a couple's chances to successfully overcome their difficulties. It also means they are more likely to survive the after-effects of handling severe problems.

Multiple Emotional Problems

Sometimes couples have to face more than one kind of psychological difficulty. Along with being codependent one partner may also suffer from an additional emotional illness. Other forms of therapy in addition to codependency treatment will probably be necessary. The love emphasis in CoRecovery work is usually very helpful in these cases of multiple emotional problems. As we have already noted, love promotes healing in many forms of illness. This is true whether the illness is physical or psychological.

Another reason for CoRecovery work is that a love problem may be at the root of the emotional illness. Dr. Rubin Fine, the eminent director of the New York Center for Psychoanalytic Training, puts it well when he says: "Regardless of what problem a person comes to an analyst with, sooner or later it becomes clear that there is a lack in their love lives, and that the problem cannot be satisfactorily resolved unless the love problem is remedied" (1985,xi). Because love problems can underlie codependency and other psychological problems, I would like to recommend that CoRecovery counseling be intermixed with the other forms of treatment when there are multiple problems.

THE CHALLENGE OF ONGOING LOVE

I want to challenge you to keep learning about love. Couples can make wonderful teams for learning about love. Finding ideas about love and sharing them, talking over concepts about love and how they apply to your relationship, and going together into love learning experiences can all enrich your life together. I remember one man who had the most awed look on his face. His CoRecovery group had been talking about the different things they had learned about love. His comment was typical. "I never dreamed there was so much to learn about love. I'm utterly astonished at how much I don't know." In our culture love ignorance is of epidemic proportions. Yet the knowledge is available for those who search for it. Therefore, it is essential that couples meet the challenge of learning about love.

I want to challenge you to practice what you learn about love. Without repeated practice, people slip back to their old habits. Only through conscientious repetition can you replace your old behaviors with new behaviors.

I want to challenge you to fully enjoy love. The wonderful feelings that flow out of healthy love are sometimes gentle, exquisite, ethereal, powerful, poignant, comforting, challenging, and beautiful, and always precious. Sometimes experiencing these feelings is especially hard for people suffering in codependency. Several authorities in the field have discussed how the factors that lead to codependency also lead to a suppression of feelings and feeling expression (Subby 1984; Myer *et al* 1991). From this flows a codependent tendency to vicariously live through other people's feelings. To meet the challenge of fully enjoying love means learning to live through your feelings.

I want to challenge you to develop full, healthful self-love. The relationship between healthy self-love and mate love seems very clear to me in working with couples. The more you healthfully love yourself, the more you will be able to love your mate. The more you love yourself, the more you will be able to accept love from your mate and others. As a part of your self-love I want to challenge you to strive to be the most you can be. The more you make of yourself, the more you have to offer your mate.

And the more you make of yourself the more you have to add to your love relationship.

Naturally I also want to challenge you to love your mate intensely, powerfully, grandly, intimately and thoroughly. If you are going to do mate love, you might as well do it well. You can always find new and wonderful ways to love your mate. Mate love is an art that can always be developed to higher forms. If you live to be two hundred you will still find new and better ways to romantically, intimately, and preciously love your mate.

May I also challenge you to love many people and let yourself be loved by many? Living as a member of a network of healthy, loving people is the best living. Money, status, power, fame, all pale by comparison to love. People search for things like money and power as substitutes for the love they are missing. The couple who lives in a network of loving people of varying kinds is the couple who lives most well.

I want to challenge you to love humanity. As species go, we humans have a lot of potential. We are a young species and are probably just getting started. There are many life forms that have been on this planet five, ten and even twenty times longer than we humans. As a young species we probably need all the love we can generate if we are going to survive. You can be a positive part of this process. When a couple acts to love humanity, it helps create a partner bond. I encourage you to take up one of humanity's many causes. The profound togetherness a couple feels from acts of altruistic love can be exceptional.

Another challenge I want to give you as a couple is to love life itself. I think it is appropriate to regard life as a precious miracle. All life, as we know it, exists in an infinitesimal nook of space. It seems we are about to fling our forms of life into the universe. Simultaneously on earth we are destroying many forms of life with both known and unknown value. Is life itself to be valued or devalued? If we love life, we will value it; if we do not we will treat life as cheap and expendable. Ultimately treating any life form as valueless may lead us to treat our life form as worthless. Indeed, in every city of our society, there are places where human life is amazingly cheap. I urge couples to do what they can to operate as a team that values and enhances life; acting to love life itself is intrinsically worthwhile. Codependency can trap couples in petty behaviors, mundane living, and agonizing, yet often trivial, conflicts. A love of life can greatly help a couple transcend the petty, the mundane and the trivial. In this type of transcendence a couple can find a sense of exalted sharing.

I also challenge couples to grow their love in ways that are spiritual, as you come to understand the word spiritual. Perhaps the most intimate and simultaneously the most awesome thing a couple can share is spirituality. For countless thousands of years humans have been concerned with the spiritual. Words like Yahweh, God, Allah, the Tao, Brahma, Om, Zen, Ying and Yang, First Cause, Life Force, Great Spirit, Nirvana and a host of others, all speak to spirituality. So does the word "love," not only in my opinion but in the words of many mystics, philosophers and theologians. Therefore, I ask you and your beloved to accept the challenge of finding your distinctive way to love spiritually.

I challenge you to model love. We all learn by example. Model your love behaviors for your children, so they won't have to fight your same love problems. Model your love behaviors for your parents, so that they too can become more loving. Model love actions for friends, co-workers, and strangers. We need all the love examples we can get. If you are going to be a couple, be a loving couple everywhere. Each of the eight major ways of behaving lovingly can be done subtly or exuberantly, depending on the situation. The point is to do them.

Yes, I challenge you to live a life of love in each of these ways. It is the main way to defeat codependency and a great many other afflictions. A life based in love ensures a life worth living. Now, one last challenge—always

GROW IN LOVE!

Appendices

A Resource Guide

COUPLES SUPPORT AND STUDY GROUPS

Recovering Couples Anonymous (RCA)
P.O. Box 27617
Golden Valley, Minnesota 55442

This was the first Twelve Step support group to emphasize a couple's relationship instead of the more usual Twelve Step accent on individuals. The main requirement is that a couple have a desire to remain in a committed relationship. Membership is open to both traditional and nontraditional couples. The group works to help couples with the development of individuality, mutual interdependent functioning and all types of recovery issues within the content of a mated relationship. RCA is relatively new having been founded in 1988 but is growing rapidly across the U.S.A.

CoRecovery Support Groups and Study Groups
The Center for Counseling and Developmental Services (CCDS)
7525 John T. White Rd.
Ft. Worth, Texas 76120
or
245 Sandy Lane
Ft. Worth, Texas 76120
(817) 429-5050

CoRecovery support groups and study groups have just begun to form. The emphasis of the support groups is on supporting couples in their efforts to live in love functional relationships. The emphasis in the study groups is to help couples and individuals learn the new and more healthful knowledge about love being discovered in ongoing research in many fields. Each group is independent and self-governing. Material for assistance in forming a CoRecovery support or study group are sent on request. I would also enjoy receiving your questions and comments about love and coRecovery.

Couples Religious Connected Support and Study Groups

Many denominations have formed various programs for assisting couples in their relationships. Too many programs exist to review them all here. Usually you need only contact your local congregation offices to see what is available. I do like to suggest that the most helpful couples groups are those in which the couple spends most of their time together as a couple. Some religious programs divide the couple for the majority of the time dealing with men in one group and women in another. This, in my opinion, is useful for individual development but not for couples teamwork development. Also let me suggest that nontraditional couples often fare best in support and study groups sponsored through Unitarian/Universalist congregations, Unity congregations and other more liberal religious denominations. These are open to couples of all religions as well as those of mixed religions, and you are not likely to be proselytized there.

CODEPENDENCY AND RELATED ISSUE GROUPS

Co-Dependents Anonymous (CoDa)
P. O. Box 33577
Phoenix, Arizona 85067-3577
(602) 277-7991

CoDa is the largest and most rapidly growing program for helping people deal with codependency. There are several thousand CoDa groups across the U.S.A. and they also exist in twelve other countries. CoDa follows a Twelve Step approach and accepts both individuals and couples in its program. The basic requirement is a desire for a healthy and loving relationship with oneself and others.

Codependents of Sex Addiction (Co-SA)
P. O. Box 14537
Minneapolis, Minnesota 55414
(612) 537-6904

Co-SA is a Twelve Step recovery program primarily for the mates of people suffering from sex addiction.

International S Anon Family Groups (S-Anon)
P. O. Box 5117
Sherman Oaks, California 91413
(818) 990-6901

S-Anon deals with the codependency issues of families and friends of sex addicts. It is allied with SA and is similar to Co-SA. It was founded in 1982 and has groups across the U.S.A., Canada and in several other countries.

Family Groups Headquarters Inc. (Al-Anon)
P. O. Box 862
Midtown Station
New York, New York 10018-0862
(212) 302-7240

Al-Anon was the first Twelve Step support group program founded to help people deal with codependency issues. Al-Anon has over 30,000 groups in over 100 countries. It is primarily for the mates, family members and friends of people who suffer from alcoholism.

Co-Anon
P. O. Box 64742-66
Los Angeles, California 90064

Co-Anon is a Twelve Step group designed to help the mates, families, and friends of cocaine addicts deal with their codependency issues. It works much like Al-Anon.

Adult Children of Alcoholics (ACA)
P. O. Box 3216
2522 W. Sepulveda Blvd. Suite 200
Torrance, California 90505
(213) 534-1815

Codependency problems are seen as particularly rampant in adults who had one or more alcoholic parents. For that reason ACA (also known as ACoA in some locations) was founded. ACA is a Twelve Step support group program whose only basic requirement for membership is identifying with the problem. ACA is rather large having over 1,500 groups spread throughout the U.S.A., Canada, Europe, and other countries. There are also special versions of ACA for homosexual men, lesbian woman, incest survivors and those who wish to go to gender separated meetings. ACA groups often include a study group component with books and other readings recommended.

Nar-Anon (Family Groups)
P. O. Box 2562
Palos Verdes, California 90274
(213) 547-5800

The codependency problems of narcotic addicts and their mates, families, and friends are addressed in this Al-Anon-like program. Nar-Anon meetings can be found all across the U.S.A., Canada, and in many other parts of the world. Nar-Anon uses a Twelve Step approach and has literature available in several languages.

Families Anonymous (FA)
P. O. Box 528
Van Nuys, California 91408
(818) 989-7841

The codependency problems of families and especially children as they relate to substance abuse are the focus in FA. Parents, grandparents and children of all ages are reached by this Twelve Step approach. This FA is not to be confused with another "FA" which stands for Fundamentalists Anonymous.

Rational Recovery Systems (RR)
P. O. Box 800
Lotus, California 95651
(916) 621-4374

COUNSELORS AND THERAPISTS

CoRecovery Counselors and Therapists

The Center for Counseling and Developmental Services (CCDS)
7525 John T. White Rd *or* 245 Sandy Lane
Ft. Worth, Texas 76120
(817) 429-5050

Appendix: A Resource Guide

A small but growing number of counselors and therapists are receiving training in the methods mentioned in this book. They work in agencies, private practices, hospitals, universities, treatment centers and clinics. Contact CCDS to find out if one is available in your area. If you are a counselor or therapist contact CCDS to see about becoming a CoRecovery counselor in your area.

Some agencies, counseling centers, training organizations and hospitals have also begun to conduct CoRecovery training sessions for their professional staff in cooperation with CCDS. Check with similar organizations in your area to see if their staff is receiving such training.

Couples Counselors and Therapists

To find a counselor who may be trained and experienced in working with couples you can consult the following organizations for referral in you local area:

American Association for Marriage and Family Therapy (AAMFT)
1717 K Street NW
Washington, D.C. 20006
(202) 429-1825

Referral source for locating highly qualified couples, marital, and family therapists in the U.S.A. and Canada.

American Association for Counseling and Development (AACD)
5999 Stevenson Ave Suite 402
Alexandria, Virginia 22304
(703) 461-6222

This source provides referrals for many types of professional counselors throughout the U.S.A., many of whom are also trained and experienced in couples work. Two of its affiliates are The National Board of Certified Counselors and the International Association of Marriage and Family Counselors at the same address as stated above.

National Association of Alcohol and Drug Abuse Counselors (NAADAC)
3717 Columbia Pike Suite 300
Arlington, Virginia 22204
(703) 920-4644 or 1-800-548-0497

Appendix: A Resource Guide

Since codependency was first discovered by people working with alcoholics, many counselors in this organization are quite knowledgeable when it comes to codependency. However, alcohol and drug abuse counselors are just beginning to learn about the specialized techniques used in couples work. If you or your mate face substance or behavioral addictions and you can not find a counselor trained in both addictions and couples work, try to find a team where both orientations are represented.

American Association of Sex Education Counselors and Therapists (AASECT)
435 N Michigan Avenue
Chicago, Illinois 60611-4067
(312) 644-0282

If there are pronounced sexual problems in a couple's or an individual's life, AASECT can provide referral to well-trained counselors and therapists in you local area.

National Association of Social Workers
National Headquarters and Publishing Office
7981 Eastern Avenue
Silver Spring, Maryland 20910

NASW can provide referrals in your area to charitable and governmental agencies which may provide low cost counseling, including couples and family treatment.

For Checking Counselor and Therapist Credentials

Consumer awareness in counseling and therapy is hard to come by. There are so many different kinds of credentials and types of counselors that it can boggle anyone's mind. To ease this problem Dick Martin, a colleague of mine, and I compiled a credentials directory. You can ask for it at you local public or college library. If they do not have it you can recommend they acquire a copy from the publisher. The particulars are: *A Directory of Credentials in Counseling and Psychotherapy* By: Daniel R. Martin and J. Richard Cookerly, Published by: G K Hall of Boston, Massachusetts in 1989.

Appendix: A Resource Guide

OTHER HELP AND SUPPORT GROUPS

National Self-Help
Clearinghouse
33 W 42nd St
New York, New York 10036
(212) 642-2944

Alcoholics Anonymous
P. O. Box 454
Grand Central Station
New York, NY 10017
(212) 686-1100

AmericanAnorexia/Bulimia
Association, Inc.
133 Cedar Ln
Teaneck, NJ 07666
(201) 836-1800

Cocaine Anonymous
World Service Office
3740 Overland Ave Suite G
Los Angeles, CA 90034
(213) 559-5833
800-347-8998

Debtors Anonymous
General Service Board
P. O. Box 20322
New York, NY 10025-9992

Drugs Anonymous
P. O. Box 473
Anson Station, NY 10023
(212) 874-0700

Emotions Anonymous
International Services
P. O. Box 4254
St. Paul, MN 55104
(612) 647-9712

Fundamentalists Anonymous
P. O. Box 20324
Greeley Square Station
New York, NY 10001
(212) 696-0420

Gam-Anon
International Service Office
P. O. Box 157
Whitestone, NY 11357
(718) 352-1671

Gamblers Anonymous
P. O. Box 17173
Los Angeles, CA 90017
(213) 386-8789

Incest Survivors Anonymous
P. O. Box 5613
Long Beach, CA 90805-0613

Marijuana Anonymous
1527 N. Washington Ave.
Scranton, PA 18509

Narcotics Anonymous
P. O. Box 9999
Van Nuys, CA 91409
(818) 780-3951

O-Anon
General Service Office
P. O. Box 4350
San Pedro, CA 90731

Overeaters Anonymous
P. O. Box 92870
Los Angeles, CA 90009
(213) 542-8363

Appendix: A Resource Guide

Parents Anonymous
22330 Hawthorne
Torrace, CA 90505
(215) 372-1128

Pill Addicts Anonymous
P. O. Box 278
Reading, PA 19603
(215) 372-1128

Sex Addicts Anonymous
P.O. Box 3038
Minneapolis, MN 55403
(612) 339-0217

Sexaholics Anonymous
P.O. Box 300
Simi Valley, CA 93062
(805) 581-3343

Sex & Love Addicts
Anonymous
Augustine Fellowship
P.O. Box 119
Newtown Branch
Boston, MA 02258
(617) 332-1845

Smokers Anonymous
2118 Greenwich St
San Francisco, CA 94123

Survivors of Incest
Anonymous
P. O. Box 21817
Baltimore, MD 21222-6817
(301) 282-3400

References

The new knowledge about love is hard to come by. It is being discovered in at least a dozen different scientific fields, but to date there is no one or primary reference source. To ease this process some of my colleagues and I have put together a cassette tape series. The basic set is called the *Course on Love* (6 tapes/ approximately 6 hours) and this is suggested for those who want to learn more about the dynamics of love. Free information about this tape series can be obtained by calling (817) 429-5050.

The References listed in this volume present a fair starting point for further learning about love. Each of the publications listed mentions other resources you can learn from. Slowly more is being published about love that makes practical sense, so keep looking.

Ard, Ben and Constance C. Ard (ed.). 1969. *Handbook of marriage counseling*. Palo Alto, Cal.: Science and Behavior Books Inc.

Bakwin, Harry and Ruth M. Bakwin. 1942. *Psychologic core during infancy and childhood*. New York: Apeleton-Century.

Beavers, Robert. 1977. *Psychotherapy and growth: A family systems perspective*. New York: Brunner/Mazel.

Beecher, M.N. 1986. Three cardiologists report prayers for their patients are "answered." *Medical Tribune* Jan 8.

Bern, Eric. 1964. *Games people play: The psychology of human relationships*. New York: Grove Press Inc.

Bern, Eric. 1988. *What do you say after you say hello: The psychology of human destiny*. New York: Grove Press Inc.

Brennemann, J. 1932. The infant ward. *American Journal of Diseases of Children* 32:577.

Brook, Byron. 1989. *Design your love life: Intimacy with independence commitment without confinement*. New York: Walker and Co.

Brown, Grant F. 1970. Divorces in and out of the counseling process. Paper presented at the Family Counseling Seminar Series, October, at the Fort Worth Neuropsychiatric Center, Fort Worth, Tex.

References

Burgess, Paul. 1985. Using nonverbal communication results in marital and family therapy: A survey of possibility. Paper presented at Southwestern Family Therapy Institute, 15 August, Austin, Tex.

Byers, E.S., S.H. Cohen, and D. Harshbarger. 1979. The quantity and quality of aftercare services: Relationship with recidivism in mental hospital patients. *Canada Journal of Behavioral Science* 11(1):11-20.

Chapin, H.D. 1915. A plea for accurate statistics in infants' institutions. *Transactions of the American Pediatric Society* 27: pp. 313-42.

Clanton, Gordon and Lynn G. Smith (ed.). 1977. *Jealousy*. Englewood Cliffs, N.J.: Prentice-Hall.

Cookerly, J. Richard. 1976. Evaluating Different Approaches to Marriage counseling. In *Treating relationships*, ed David H.L. Olson, 475-98, Lake Mills, Iowa: Graphic Publishing Co.

Cookerly, J. Richard. 1980. Does marital therapy do any lasting good? *Journal of Marital and Family Therapy* 6(4):393-98.

Cookerly, J. Richard, and Kathleen McClaren. 1982. Sex therapy with and without love: An empirical investigation. *Journal of Sex Education and Therapy* 8(2):35-54.

Cookerly, J. Richard and Kathleen McClaren. 1986. Love behavior training for sex counselors and therapists: A way toward improvemcnt. *Journal of Sex Education and Therapy* 12(1):51-54.

Diamond, Marian. 1983. *How the brain grows in response to experience*. Los Altos, Cal.: Institute for the Study of Human Knowledge.

Ferm, Vergilius T. (ed.) 1985. *An encyclopedia of religion*. New York: Philosophical Library

Fine, Rubin. 1985. *The meaning of love in human experience*. New York: John Wiley and Sons.

Fried, Ralph, and M.F. Mayer. 1948. Socio-emotional factors accounting for growth failure of children living in an institution. *Journal of Pediatrics* 33:444-46.

Gibran, Kahlil. 1923. *The prophet*. New York: Alfred A. Knopf.

Gillies, Jerry. 1978. *Transcendental sex: A meditative approach to increasing sexual pleasure*. New York: Holt Rineheart and Winston.

Glaser, R., J. Kiecolt-Glaser, J.M. George, C.E. Speicher and J.E. Holliday. 1984. Stress loveliness and herpes virus latency. Paper presented at the conference of the Society of Behavioral Medicine, May, at Philadelphia, Pa.

Gore, Samuel. 1978. The effects of social support in moderating the health consequences of unemployment. *Journal of Health and Social Behavior* 19:157-65.

Gurman, Allen S. and D.P. Kniskern. 1981. *Handbook of family therapy*. New York: Brunner/Mazel.

References

Gurman, Chiristine 1991. Are gay men born that way? *Time* 138(10):60-61.

Hamburg, D.A., G. Elliot and D. Parron (eds.). 1982. *Health and behavior: Frontiers of research in the biobehavioral sciences*. Washington D.C.: National Academy Press.

Harlow, Harry F. and M.K. Harlow. 1965. The affectional systems. In *Behavior of nonhuman primates* Vol II, ed. A.M. Schrier, H.F. Harlow and F. Stollnitz, New York: Academic Press.

Harlow, Harry F. 1971. *Learning to love*. San Francisco: Albino Publishing Co.

Hogg, James A., and Mary Lou Granks. 1992. Toward an interpersonal model of codependence and contradependence. Journal of Counseling and Development 70 (3): 371-382.

Hopson, J.L. 1984. A love affair with the brain: A PT conversation with Marion Diamond. *Psychology Today* 11:70.

Horton, William J. 1990. Personality correlates of intolerance in certain physically abusive perpetrators. Paper presented at Tarrant County Juvenile Offenders Seminar, 7 March, Ft. Worth, Tex.

Jackobson, N.S. 1978. A review of the research on the effectiveness of marital therapy. In *Marriage and family therapy: Psychoanalytic behavioral and systems theory perspectives*, ed. T.J. Paolino and B.S. McCrady, 132-40, New York: Brunner/Mazel.

Justice, Blair. 1988. *Who gets sick?* Los Angeles: Jeremy Tarcher.

Kant, Immanuel. 1934. Religion within the limits of reason alone. Trans. by T. M. Green and H. H. Hudson. Chicago: Open Court Publishing Co.

Kaplan, Helen Singer. 1974. *The new sex therapy: Active treatment of sexual dysfunctions*. New York: Brunner/Mazel.

Karlen, Arno. 1988. *Threesomes: Studies in sex power and intimacy*. New York: Beach Tree Books.

Kassorla, Irene. 1976. *Putting it all together*. New York: Warner Books.

Laign, J. 1989. A consensus on codependency. *Contact* 2 (2):2.

Langdon-Davies, John. 1927. *A short history of women*. New York: Literary Guild of America.

Langer, E. J. and J. Rodin. 1976. The effects of choice and enhanced personal responsibility for the age: A field experiment in an institutional setting. *Journal of Personality and Social Psychology* 34: 191-98.

LeVay, Simon 1991. A difference in hypothalamic structure between heterosexual and homosexual men. *Science* 253: 1034-37.

References

Lewis, Jerry, Robert Beavers, John Gossett, and V.A. Phillips. 1976. *No single thread: Psychological health in family systems*. New York: Brunner/Mazel.

Locke, Steven E. (ed.). 1986. *Psychological and behavioral treatments for disorders associated with the immune system: An annotated bibliography*. New York: Institute for the Advancement of Health.

Lyon, Quinter M. 1957. *The great religions*. New York: Odyssey Press.

Marlatt, G.A. and J.R. Gordon. 1980. Determinants of relaps: Implications for the maintenance of behavior change. In *Behavioral medicine: hanging health lifestyles*, ed. P.O. Davidson and S.M. Davidson, 97-123. New York: Brunner/Mazel.

Martin, Daniel and J. Richard Cookerly. 1989. *A directory of credentials in counseling and psychotherapy*. Boston: G.K Hall and Co.

Maslow, Abraham H. 1970. *Motivation and personality* rev. ed. New York: Harper and Row.

Mason, Marilyn. 1988. Sexuality issues during recovery. In *Codependency*, ed Editors Magazine, 65-70. Dearfield Beach, Fla: Health Communications Inc.

Masters, William H. and Virginia E. Johnson. 1970. *Human sexual inadequacy*. Boston: Little Brown and Co.

McCrady, Barbara S., Nora E. Noel, David B. Abrams, Robert L. Stout, Hiller Fisher Nelson, and William M. Hay. 1986. Comparative effectiveness of three types of spouse involvement in outpatient behavioral alcoholism treatment. *Journal of Studies on Alcohol* 47(6):459-466.

Mellody, Pia, Andrea Wells Miller and J. Keith Miller. 1989. *Facing codependence: What it is, where it comes from, how it sabotages our lives*. San Francisco: Harper and Row.

Mellon, Sydney. 1981. *The evolution of love*. San Francisco: W.H. Freeman and Company.

Miller, J.A. 1986. Immunity and crises, large and small. *Science News* May 31.

Montagu, Ashley. 1975. *The practice of love*. Englewood Cliffs, N.J.: Prentice-Hall.

Myer, Rick A., Sara E. Peterson, and Michele Stoffel-Rosales. 1991. Codependency examination of underlying assumptions. *Journal of Mental Health Counseling* 13(4):449-58.

Nerem, R.M., M.J. Levesque and J.F. Cornhill. 1980. Social environment as a factor in diet induced atherosclerosis. *Science* 208(44-52):1475-76.

References

Nuckolls, K.B., June Cassel and Beverly H. Kaplan. 1972. Psychosocial assets, life crisis and the prognosis of pregnancy. *American Journal of Epidemiology* 95(5):431-41.

O'Farrell, Timothy J., Henry S.G. Cutter, and Frank J. Floyd. 1985. Evaluating behavioral marital therapy for male alcoholics: effects on marital adjustment and communication before and after treatment. *Behavior Therapy* 16(1):147-167.

O'Regan B. 1985. Positive emotions: The emerging science of feelings. Paper presented at the conference on How might positive emotions effect physical health, 15-18 March, at the Institute for the Advancement of Health, New York City, NY.

Olson, David H., C.S. Russell, and D.H. Sprenkle. 1980. Marital and family therapy: A Decade review. *Journal of Marriage and the Family* 42:973-993.

Paul I *Corinthians*. King James Version.

Pedersen, Paul B. (ed.). 1991. Special issue: Multiculturalism as a fourth force in counseling. *Journal of Counseling and Development* 70(1):4-250.

Pransky, George. 1990. *Divorce is not the answer: A change of heart will save your marriage*. Blue Ridge Summit, Pa.: HSI/TAB Books-McGraw-Hill.

Russell, Jon T. 1978. Possible psychophysical origins of varying gender preferences in the offspring of laboratory animal populations. Paper presented at Interface Symposium, 26 September, at Dallas, Tex.

Selye, Hans. 1976. *The stress of life*. Rev. ed. New York: McGraw-Hill.

Shulman, Gerald. 1988. Sexuality and recovery. In *Codependency*, ed. Focus Magazine, 75-79. Dearfield Beach, Fla.: Health Communications Inc.

Siegel, Bernie S. 1986. *Love medicine and miracles*. New York: Harper and Row.

Siegel, Bernie. 1989. *Peace, love and healing*. New York: Harper and Row.

Siegman, A. W. and S. Feldstein. 1985. The relationship of expressive vocal behavior and severity of coronary artery disease. Paper presented at the meeting of the Society of Behavioral Medicine, March, New Orleans, LA.

Spitz, Rene. 1947. Anaclitic depression. *The Psychoanalytic Study of The Child* 2:313-42.

Subby, Robert. 1984. Inside the chemically dependent marriage: Denial and manipulation. In *Codependency*, ed. Focus Magazine, 25-29. Dearfield Beach, Fla: Health Communication Inc.

Swenson, Clifford H. 1972. The behavior of love. In *Love today: A new exploration*, ed. Herbert A. Otto, 87-101, New York: Dell Publishing Co.

References

Talbot, N.B., E.H. Sabel, B.S. Burke, E. Lindemann and S.S. Kaufman. 1947. Dwarfism in healthy children: Its possible relation to emotional disturbances. *New Englewood Journal of Medicine* 236:783-93.

Talbot, N.B. et al. 1947. Dwarfism in healthy children: Its possible relation to emotional disturbances. *New England: Journal of Medicine* 236:783-93.

Thomas, P.D., Jim Goodwin, Jane Goodwin. 1985. Effects of social support on stress related changes in cholesterol level in uric acid level and immune function in an elderly couple. *American Journal of Psychiatry* 142(6):735-37.

Thomas, Ruth. 1983. The need to reconceptualize homosexuality: A review of port theories and empirical evidence. Paper presented at the Applied Clinical Research Colloquium of the North Texas Association of Psychotherapists, 19 February, at the University of Texas at Arlington, Arlington, Tex.

Vobejda, Barbara. 1991. Reports says fewer marrying: Divorce cohabitation rates increase significantly. *The Washington Post*, Washington D.C. 23 August.

Williams, R. 1985. Approaches to alternation of type A behavior pattern. Paper presented at the meeting of the Society of Behavioral Medicine, March, New Orleans, LA.

Zweben, Allen, Sheldon Pearlman and Selina Li. 1988. A comparison of brief advice and conjoint therapy in the treatment of alcohol abuse: The results of the marital systems study. *British Journal of Addiction* 83(1):899-916.

About the Author

Dr. J. Richard Cookerly has been in full-time private practice, specializing in marriage, family and related relationship problems for more than twenty years. During that time he has worked with more than a thousand couples facing what are now called *codependency issues*. Since 1974, he has also been Clinical Director of a multidisciplinary counseling center, and since 1980, Clinical Professor of Psychotherapy at the University of Texas at Arlington. Licensed in Texas, he has numerous postgraduate credentials and honors, including Fellow and Diplomat of the American Board of Medical Psychotherapists, Clinical Member and Approved Supervisor of the American Association of Marital and Family Therapists. He is an experienced seminar leader, lecturer, and talk show guest.

